WHAT

GOD

HAS DONE TO US, THROUGH US, AND FOR US

MELODY HALL

ISBN 978-1-0980-2513-7 (paperback)
ISBN 978-1-0980-4515-9 (hardcover)
ISBN 978-1-0980-2514-4 (digital)

Christian Faith Publishing, Inc.
832 Park Avenue
Meadville, PA 16335
www.christianfaithpublishing.com

Printed in the United States of America

CONTENTS

PREFACE

Just the Facts!

A Preamble Behind the Book

This book has been more than thirty years in the making. I have been wanting to write this book to help others make it through their own journey. Life is never the same from one person to another, much less families!

This book is a big story full of little stories of the amazingness of our God. This book is about a few of the things God has done to us, through us, and for us. Some say, "He doesn't do miracles anymore!" Others, "He doesn't speak [audibly] to us anymore." Several don't believe there are angels that we can see, talk with, or touch. And still many have a deep yearning in their hearts and minds for the God of the Bible that did all those amazing things for the children of Israel all those millennia ago to do something—anything—for them sometime in this lifetime. Well, this book is to let you know that He did, He does, and He will. We are no better than others, and He did it—still does it for us! He is not a respecter of persons; His word says that. My prayer is that you will be blessed, inspired, and caused to *dare* to believe and hope within a hope that He *will* do it for you for His glory!

Steve and I have been married now for over thirty-two years; and though the stories are in chronological order, there are many, many more stories of the things God has done just in our family alone within the timeline that these stories took place! These stories are all one hundred percent true from beginning to end. I have changed the names of a few of the people in the stories for their privacy; some, I have lost track of over the years and haven't been able to find them to get permission to tell their part of our story; while still a few, I never knew their names to begin with.

I pray this book is the catalyst that causes you to seek God at a much deeper level and to learn for yourself just how much God loves you and will do many amazing, miraculous things just to you, through you, and for you!

INTRODUCTION

All About Us

I was born Melody Noelle Nettles on March 10, 1969 in Upland, California, to Rev. Darrell Eugene and Beverly Diane Nettles. It was on my dad's twenty-fifth birthday! I was the most expensive present he ever got! I was born five months before dad was in the same hospital on the third floor in traction due to a serious accident at his work at the Alpha Beta Grocery Store warehouse.

My brother David was born on June 18, 1965, which happened to be Father's Day that year. My dad was a very blessed man! We lived in Ontario, California, until just after all of my sisters were born. My parents had us four girls and our older brother, and we all lived in a little white two-bedroom house with one bathroom at 904 S. San Antonio Avenue in Ontario. The siblings in our family were my brother David, me, Heather (1973), Antoinette (1975), and Charity (1977; she was just five days from being born on our birthday).

I was originally going to be named "Faith," but when they were deciding, God very clearly spoke to my parents and told them my name was to be "Melody Noelle." They were hoping to have a "Faith, Hope, and Charity," but they ended up only getting the "Charity" out of that name bunch. It truly is fitting; I sing all the time! I'm either singing fully out loud, humming, singing quietly under my breath, whistling, or singing in my head.

When I was born, I had a huge issue around my stomach that almost cost me my life; but after the doctors gave up and wanted to

7

do surgery, my dad and mom said, "No, give us a day to pray. And then if it's still needed, we will consent."

So they did. They "prayed heaven down," as the saying for Pentecostals go. God moved and showed the answer to our family doctor. He came up with a medication that they had to give me thirty minutes before I could eat, and then only feed me small amounts. I was hungry all the time. Mom would give me the medicine, wait the thirty minutes while I screamed for hunger, and start to feed me. But I would guzzle so fast, I would get sick or gag, then she'd stop feeding me for a while and do it all over again. She was doing the "feeding baby" cycle continuously, it seemed. It did work, however; and as my body grew and "caught up" with the size of the muscle that was above my stomach, the need for the medicine went away, and she was able to feed me without any more issues. Praise God! The devil has been trying to take me out since birth!

My family moved to Tucson in June of 1978 because my sister Antoinette has severe asthma and spent most of her first two years in the hospital instead of at home with the family. After the last really bad asthma attack in the spring of 1978, our family doctor, Dr. Dest, told my dad that if he expected my sister to live to see her next birthday, he needed to get her out of California. Dad asked him, if it were his daughter, where would he move his family to? Dr. Dest answered immediately without any hesitation, "Tucson, Arizona." We were loading a truck and moving to our new home dad had found in Tucson just two weeks later.

On Saturday, two weeks after we arrived (which took us three days, by the way, instead of ten hours), I was playing at the park just a block away with one of our neighbor girls. We were on the steel teeter-totter with no back-brace thing when I slipped off. I immediately jumped up and opened my mouth to yell for my brother to catch the teeter-totter to keep my side from going up, hitting me when it did just that! It hit me and knocked my top right front tooth, root and all, right out of my mouth! We found the tooth and ran it to the water fountain to wash it off and maybe try to put it back. A dentist was there playing ball with his son and told me not to do that but to keep it wet and take it to a dentist's office where it can be done properly. He left and never gave his name.

When we got home, I was a mess with blood everywhere. After we told our mom and dad what happened and gave them the tooth, my dad went into their room and cried. I didn't know that until many years later. With us being brand-new to the area, we had no idea about emergency dental offices or even dentists in general, so we could not get in until Monday. By that time, it was way too late to reattach the tooth, so I ended up getting a partial plate. Most people call them "flipper plates." It is only to be used as a temporary fix, but I ended up having it for over twenty years.

While our kids were young, before I was able to get the bridge, we would have sleepovers and parties and such when I would totally freak out the other kids by eating with them and causing my false tooth to go flying across the table toward the guest kid. *Wow!* The looks of astonishment and squeals and screams from those kids and other interesting reactions were priceless! While I utterly enjoyed it, my kids were rolling their eyes and glaring at me. Of course, I only did it when we had kids that were pretty much adopted into the family, not just complete strangers getting to know or see us for the first time.

The dentist that was finally able to put in a permanent bridge was Dr. David Schram in Bemidji, Minnesota, in 2001. The partial plate did its damage to the roof or palette of my mouth, but he fought with our insurance and got my mouth healthy. He did a *beautiful* job! Even now in 2019, I get compliments on it from dentists and even passersby that don't know about my bridge!

I wasn't the only ornery one around, so don't think ill of just me! Steve would tell stories to the kids at night. They were always the "haunted house" and spooky ones. The kids' all-time favorite was "The Wet Bandit!" What a hoot! It became his "signature" story when we got involved in kids ministries and Royal Rangers. Everyone got wet when he told that story, and I mean everyone! Cups of water went flying everywhere; *no one* was safe!

We were also *notorious* for having water fights. Let me just say that our water wars were epic! They left inches of water inside the house/apartments we stayed at. Yes, *inside*, but that was no comparison to the outside! We used hoses, huge pails, cups, pitchers, whatever was handy! If you were involved, you were drenched by the end. There was no such thing as a "safe zone" either. Well, okay, if you were near the TV; or if we had a computer, electronics, etc., we would hold back, but we called those areas "off limits!"

Okay, so enough about me. My amazing husband, Steven Daniel Hall, was born in Wadena, Minnesota, to Milton and Rose Hall. But when he was eighteen months old, his family moved to Tacoma, Washington, in the Pacific Northwest. He grew up in Washington, though in various western Washington areas. He was the youngest boy of seven boys, and then they had the two girls. He actually had another sister that was born second in the family line of siblings, but she passed away at three months old from pneumonia and was buried in Bemidji, Minnesota. His oldest brother, Al, was born pretty close to the same year my dad was.

When Steve was a senior in high school, he, his parents, and sisters moved down to Tucson, Arizona, where he only had to take one class to graduate. He chose PE, of all things. He had it first period so he could get his workout in, shower, then head off to work at Church's Chicken near St. Mary's Hospital. They loved the weather, but after Steve graduated, they all moved back up to Washington.

Steve was only up there for a little while, and then he moved back to Tucson, Arizona. He worked hard and became an assistant manager of the Church's Chicken at Ajo and Sixth Avenue. It was the busiest store in the US back in the late 1980s. It's no longer at that location; they moved it up a couple of blocks on Sixth Avenue. That is where he was working when God brought us together.

So enter into the following pages with your seatbelts fastened, keep your hands and feet in at all times until this ride comes to a safe and complete stop! Let the fun begin!

CHAPTER 1

Arranged Marriage

*W*hen I was twelve, my best friend was Michele. We were inseparable. So much so that one Sunday, I went with her to her church, which at that time was on the southwest side of Tucson near Old Tucson; and then the next week, she came with me to mine at East Tucson Church of God.

One day, I was at her church, and I heard God's voice in my ear say, "Do you see that guy over there?" And my eyes immediately went to this particular young man with longer hair than my parents would have approved of at the front of the church with a few other guys. I asked, "That guy?" to which God replied, "Yes, that guy. He is going to be your husband." I looked at him a bit and thought to myself, *Cool.* I then went about the rest of my day.

Over the next two weeks, however, my conversations were continually loaded with "Steve this and Steve that" as Michele and I talked. She got utterly sick of hearing about how wonderful Steve was. She thought the whole thing about God's telling me he would be my husband was awesome, but I was driving her nuts with "Steve, Steve, Steve!"

The next time I was at her church, she had me up by the elbow before the pastor said, "Amen!" to his benediction and was dragging me up to the front where Steve stood, talking with his friends, and threw me into his chest. She said, "Steve, this is Melody. Melody, this is Steve. Now you can shut up and stop talking about him all the time!" at which point, she proceeded to turn around and march away, leaving me in his arms. I was so utterly embarrassed; I could've crawled home across town!

He looked down at me, wondering what he could say that wouldn't make my embarrassment worse and came up with a very good idea. "So, do you like 'Judas' Kiss'?"

Instantly, in my head, I began to question God in His infinite wisdom about this guy who likes satanic music. Somehow, Steve seemed to know my thoughts about the music and said, "Not Judas Priest the band but 'Judas' Kiss,' a song by a Christian rock band called Petra."

When I shook my head, he proceeded to grab his "ghetto blaster," plopped it unceremoniously down *onto the altar*, and blasted the hard rock song right there *in the sanctuary!* I immediately began to back up, knowing that lightning was going to strike any minute, and I was *not* going to be zapped along with this person committing sacrilege in church.

After several minutes and no lightning, I began to really think about the song itself. I could understand every single word, and it really did talk about Jesus and what sacrifice He made for us. *Wow!* It was pretty powerful.

Over the next several years, we became good friends, especially since he dated almost every one of my single older girlfriends. I have always been a "Dear Abby" for anyone who needed me, and my friends needed me. How they expected to have that relationship work out when God had already said he would be *my* husband is beyond me! Oh, well, I guess because God told *me* alone and not anyone else, including Steve at this particular time. I truly gave them the best advice I could, though I knew it was a doomed relationship with him from their beginning. Then he dated Theresa. She was one of my best friends.

There were four of us: Michelle T., Michele D., Theresa, and I. Anyway, they went out for a while, and next thing I knew, he left! He was gone six months, and while gone, he prayed that God would remove the garbage from his memory, and He did! God actually did a memory swipe of a few months.

While he was gone, Theresa and Michelle were walked home by my then boyfriend Billy (William J.), who had just come back from being gone to his brother's house in Boston for the summer. We were all at my house catching up since his absence and left at the same time. I went one way to babysit, and they went the other to Theresa's house because it was way after dark. Well, let's just say that he stayed for a very long while with both of them at Theresa's house in her room.

A few days later, after they had all been avoiding me like the plague, I ended up in the bathroom at the same time as Michelle. She felt cornered and started sobbing and told me the whole story. I forgave them and tried to continue with life. A week later, Billy came over and apologized and then said that he and Theresa knew that I knew about their fling. He said he wanted to break up because I was being "too nice about the whole thing!" He said that he couldn't take it knowing that I knew, and yet I treated them all just the same as I had always treated them. It drove him nuts; and when I told him that I forgave them and him for his part, he told me not to. He said he couldn't be my boyfriend knowing that he "didn't deserve me." Those three stopped coming around me after that.

During this time, my dad started acting very weird. He had mood swings that made a menopausal woman look calm. I couldn't understand how my dad was behaving and how fast he could change. He, being a mighty minister of the Gospel of Jesus Christ since he was a youth, never ever acted this way. *Ever!* It was stressing all of us at home; and then of course, the breakup with my boyfriend and two of my best friends—I was really feeling low.

Things happened that summer that was unbelievable. I actually planned for my suicide. I was going to do it two different ways so that medical staff would see the one and work on that, thinking it was more emergent at that moment when in reality, it would've been the secondary attempt. I was set and even told God that unless I had someone here on earth to help me with all this stuff, I was going to end it the Friday after Thanksgiving 1985.

The weekend before Thanksgiving, Michele D. called and asked if I'd like to come to Christian Skate Night at Rollers Skating Rink on Alvernon Road on Monday night. I said, "I'd love to," and Mom gave me permission. I figured it was a chance to have fun "one last time."

When we got there, I couldn't believe it! Steve was the DJ for the night! I ran up and gave him a hug and asked when he got back. He said he'd been back for over a month, and that it was good to see me. I looked him in the eye and said, "You owe me a couple skate!"

He said, "You got it. The first one tonight."

That couple skate changed our lives forever! While we were skating, I was skating backward; and as we talked, God spoke audibly to Steve and told him that he was skating with his future wife! Steve darn near killed us both, tripping us up when he heard that voice. Looking back, it was funny.

He asked me to go out with the group, including Michele and her sister Gretchen, that night for burgers and shakes at JB's on Broadway. My dad gave me permission when I called. Steve himself brought me home after that and asked me to go on a date with him that coming Friday, *the* Friday I was planning to end it all.

Come to find out, Steve told me several years later that he had planned on taking the deposit from the Church's Chicken on Ajo Way after work that Friday, which is their biggest money night of the week, if God didn't reveal Himself to him in a mighty way and give him a mate that would help him on this walk as a Christian. He was going to take it and disappear in Mexico, South America, or find a small island. He also told me that when I had come up to him at the DJ booth that Monday night, he vaguely remembered me at all.

That date was wonderful. It was a movie I can't remember and dinner at McDonald's, but we talked and talked. I had to be home by 11:00 p.m. and actually got home at 10:45 p.m. However, we remained seated in the yellow Ford Galaxy 200 in the driveway talking more. Every time we started to get out of the car, one of us would bring up something that really caught the interest of the other one, and we'd just keep talking.

Finally, the porch light started being flicked on and off to warn me to get in the house. As I opened the door, Steve said something else, and guess what? Yes! We started talking again! That poor light got flickered so often, it blew the bulb, and I knew I was in trouble. I had thought it was Mom reminding me to get in the house, but it was Dad!

Right before I went inside the house, Steve asked me if I'd go with him to a Christian artist named Michele Pillar's concert the next night. I told him I'd love to *if* I wasn't grounded for being outside with him until almost 12:30 a.m. Well, I was grounded all right for two weeks! My mom was livid that we stayed in his car and not in the house. So when he called the next day, I had to tell him I couldn't go with him. He called a friend and gave them the two tickets and then called his boss to work a double shift, which he did. He said later that he didn't want to go anywhere without me, and he had felt horrible for my getting in trouble. From that time on, Steve was pretty much a permanent fixture at the house. He was over every day. He played games or watched movies with the family, helped with chores, ran errands—whatever was needed to be done while he was there.

Dad had actually spent that Thanksgiving in the hospital at St Joseph's. He had been shopping at Kmart on Sunday and started complaining of shortness of breath and severe chest pain. He took himself to the hospital as Mom didn't drive. They sent him home three times that week. On Tuesday night, he went in; and this time, they admitted him for suspected pneumonia. He stayed in that hospital room until Friday morning. The X-rays all showed something in the lungs, and every doctor said it was fluid; thus, the pneumonia diagnosis.

I spent that Wednesday taking care of him in the hospital instead of going to school. It was so good having him home that Friday. Dad and I were always very close. I was born on his twenty-fifth birthday. I was his first daughter and the first baby born after he and Mom had a miscarriage between my older brother and me. We were a lot alike, and I loved spending time with him.

Three weeks after our first official date, Steve was at my house and got down on one knee in front of my dad and mom and asked me to marry him. I said, "Yes!" That was right before Christmas; and on New Year's Day, my adopted family in Phoenix, John and Liz and their three sons, would come down, and we'd "do Christmas" together and have the feast, and all the kids would go to the nearby park and play a game of football in the afternoon.

That particular football game was the bloodiest game I've ever played, and it was all my blood! Their oldest son, John Jr., known as JT, had thought that we were going to get married for a while and had decided to ask me officially on that New Year's Day with Steve there. Steve saw the ring, calmly got up, and left the house without saying a word. The football game was a couple of hours later. I took some tackles that broke my glasses, which cut the bridge of my nose and just about cracked a few ribs by getting in between those two. When they saw me bleeding, that escalated things even more. That was the absolute *worst* New Year's Day *ever* at that point.

Right after this, my parents thought we were spending way too much time together, and that I was neglecting my family. They wanted us to not go out for a while but stay around the house if we wanted to see each other because they wanted to see me and him as well. I told him on the phone just before I had to go to a babysitting job that night. He thought I was breaking up with him and ended up putting his fist through a wall at his apartment. He came over to where I was babysitting in tears and was trying to make right whatever he had done wrong. I finally got him to realize that I was *not* breaking up with him, just that my parents wanted me home more, but he was welcome to be at my house too. He was so excited! I helped to clean up his knuckles and put ice on them, and then he went home, promising to be at my house tomorrow after he got off of work.

That was the beginning of "*us.*" You could truly say that we had an "arranged marriage," arranged by the creator of marriage at that! It is so important that people really learn to listen to and for His voice. He still speaks to us today, even audibly sometimes! He already had our spouse in mind as He created each of us in the womb! He has a perfect design for every one of our lives, if only we would allow Him to rule and reign over our life! That would certainly fix a ton of the problems we make for ourselves every day.

We have now been married over thirty-two years so far and are still in love with each other and both chasing after God! No, it hasn't been an easy journey, as this book will show, but it has been a journey we have taken together.

May I be the first to introduce to you Mr
and Mrs Steven Hall (January 1987)

CHAPTER 2

Angels on the Highway

November 1987

*I*n July 1987, we had moved to Roy, Washington, truly feeling that it was God's will for us to do so. Steve had a "guaranteed" job, and his parents were going to let us stay in their little Airstream trailer on some property that belonged to two of his brothers, Mike and Richard, in the woods. We just had to supply the propane and our food.

Well, we got up there, and the "guaranteed" job gave his position away the day before he was to go in. They said that they weren't able to wait for him after all—sorry. We were devastated to say the least. Now, what were we going to do? I was about five months pregnant and showing like I was nine months, and we had just moved there, so we didn't know anyone in any jobs.

So Steve did what he could and finally found a job in another fast-food chain, Taco Bell, instead of the Church's Chicken he had left to move. He had been working for Church's Chicken since he was sixteen and was an assistant manager at the time we left Tucson. He enjoyed working for Taco Bell, and so did I. They loved trying new menu item ideas out and used me as their taster. I must say, I enjoyed his job more than he did.

This was the first time I had ever been away from my family. It was extremely difficult as I knew no one, was pregnant for the first time, dad had been gone less than a year, and I was a newlywed. I was quite homesick and missing my mom very much. Steve wanted to try to help, so knowing all of my family members are big movie buffs, he decided to take me to a movie to distract me from my homesickness.

It was mid-August, and the romantic teen comedy *Can't Buy Me Love*, starring Patrick Dempsey and Amanda Peterson, came out. It looked fun, so he took me to see it. About ten minutes into the movie, he realized what a very, very bad idea it was. While watching it, I mentioned a couple of times that a particular scene looked like this place in Tucson. Then the kicker happened: one of the big scenes was at the very mall that I had bought my wedding dress, Tucson Mall *in* Tucson, Arizona! Of all the luck! He had chosen a funny movie that I was sure to like, but it had been filmed in its entirety *in* Tucson. Needless to say, when it was over, I was even more homesick. He was so bummed. I tried to cheer him up, saying that it was still a funny, clean movie that I truly had enjoyed, and it got me out of that little, tiny Airstream trailer.

The day before Labor Day, we had to do a deep cleaning on the inside of the store as they were having a huge white glove inspection. The manager's husband and I were using toothbrushes to scrub the edges around all the baseboards along the floor throughout the whole building and above the windows while she and Steve did the scrubbing in the kitchen and storage areas. We were there from the time they closed and left about 3:00 a.m. totally exhausted.

Throughout the night, they kept teasing me that I just might go into labor on Labor Day, to which I said, "No way." I wasn't due for a few more months. However, I was feeling back pain and some slight cramping along the abdomen when we drove the forty-five-minute drive home. We actually got stopped going through Fort Lewis by the police. He looked at me, and Steve told him that I wasn't feeling well, and he was trying to get me into my bed to rest, so he let us go with a warning for speeding and said that he gets off at 7:00 a.m., so if we need a police escort to the hospital, come through this area and he would escort us. How sweet! We got home and into bed just before 4:00 a.m.

At exactly 4:00 a.m., I had this immense urge to pee. I flew to the toilet, and my water broke, plug and all! Steve was shocked. He said if he knew I had to go that bad, he would've kept speeding to get me home sooner. I told him that I didn't have to pee, but my water had broken. He wanted to know if we had to leave for the hospital now; but after I waited for the labor contractions and pain to hit, nothing happened, so I said, "No, we can go to sleep. And when I'm having contractions and pain, we'll head to Seattle to the UW Hospital as planned."

We slept till about 9:30 a.m. At 10:00, I noticed that the amniotic fluid was still trickling, so I went to Richard's wife, Cathy, my sister-in-law next door, to get a pad to use. She looked at me and said, "You're pregnant. Why do you need a pad?"

When I told her that my water broke that morning at 4:00, she about had a coronary! "What? You get in here and call your doctor right this minute!"

I tried to tell her that I wasn't in labor or having any pain, so I didn't need to bother him, but she insisted. When I told the nurse what had happened that day, she flipped out and said that we had to get in there right that minute! I informed her I lived about an hour away, and she said I need to get in there as soon as possible and to leave immediately. So I went home and told Steve what she said and then, since we worked all night, we took a shower. And of course we were starving, so I cooked some rice, not the "minute" kind either.

I finished packing my "mommy bag" for the hospital stay, and we finally got to the hospital about 1:00 p.m. They were very irritated with us for taking that long for us to get there; but when I found out I couldn't eat anything from that time till the baby was born, I was glad I took the time and ate. Of course, Steve had to have a "Big Mac attack" from McDonald's later and ate it in my room.

I wasn't in labor at all, so they had to start inducing me. We were told when it was all over that they actually had to give me three times more than they usually do.

After about 6:00 p.m., I started having issues with septicemia. I was running an infection, and it was a bad one. I actually don't remember much of the rest of the night, except that when I woke up several times, usually to puke, Steve was sitting close to my bed, holding my hand, and sometimes with his head on my bed next to me. That man would hold those little puke containers (the little pink ones that were in the shape of a kidney and were worthless to catch the vomit when there was any force behind it) while I puked, and then he'd clean me and the room up. He was so worried.

I found out a few days later that the doctor actually pulled him out of the room and told him that I wasn't expected to make it unless they give me this very strong antibiotic. *But* if they do, the antibiotic would most likely kill the baby. What did Steve want them to do, administer the drug or wait until the baby was born and try to do it then? But that would probably be way too late. Steve told them to give me the med now. He then prayed for God's protection over both me and the baby. So when I woke up, it was while I was in active labor and getting to the point of having to push. I had turned the corner and was expected to be okay.

Once Mary was born, they allowed us to hold her for a few minutes then whisked her to the NICU. She was nine pounds nine and one-half ounces with beautiful blond hair and blue-green eyes just like me. She was perfect!

When we went to visit her, it was interesting. Here was this very large baby in the NICU surrounded by these babies that could fit in your hand. She was the talk of the hospital for the week. They couldn't believe how big she was; and what's more, they couldn't believe she showed absolutely no signs of my having that antibiotic. God had completely protected her! Thank You, Jesus! I was released on Wednesday, and she was able to come home Friday afternoon. God is good!

A few days after she was born, my milk supply came in with a vengeance. I flooded my clothes with milk regularly throughout each day and most definitely every night! I had completely stuffed the little fridge in the trailer with Playtex Nurser bags full of milk besides what I was able to feed her with. We barely had any room for a few groceries like regular whole milk and eggs for us.

After two months of mass production of breast milk, I woke up one morning in November as dry as the Sahara Desert! Not one more drop was produced for her. Thank God for providing WIC, a program for nutrition for women, infants, and children. They supplied food for me while I was breastfeeding, and then cans of baby formula for Mary after my milk stopped producing. It was such a blessing!

When November came around, the business in Taco Bell switched things around, and Steve was not being treated well at his job. The manager was the same, but the regional manager had changed, and he was not the nicest of people. We had been praying and felt that we were released to go back to Tucson. It would take a couple of days to get there, what with our having to stop regularly to feed and change Mary, but that's the way it was. We didn't have any money to stay at a hotel/motel, so we planned on driving as far as we could, then pulling over at a rest stop for as long as we needed, then back on the road until we arrived in Tucson at my old house with my family.

We got into Northern California, and it was dark, late, and we were very tired. I was driving, and Steve had me pull into the next rest stop. That rest stop was as packed as I've ever seen. Every single parking spot was taken, and even trucks' spots were full, and they were lining the on-ramp onto the interstate. I pulled our little car in between two semis, got out to ensure I was well off the road. I remember thinking I felt like the filling in an Oreo cookie between the two trucks where I was.

As I got back into my car, I noticed that nothing was coming into the rest stop or trying to leave it. I rolled the front windows down about an inch, locked our doors, set our "Big Ben" alarm clock for 3:00 a.m., laid my seat back as far as possible, and started to doze off. Suddenly, lights penetrated my eyelids, and a man was knocking on my window saying, "Excuse me, but I have to get on the road, and your car is sticking out, blocking my way. Would you please move to the next rest stop? I'm sorry, but I really have to get on the road."

I sat up, told him that I would. "I'm sorry for hogging up the road. Give me a second to get the car rolling again." I assured him we had just stopped, so it wasn't like he was waking us up. He seemed relieved and followed me onto the interstate.

Now, when you get on an interstate late night/early morning, cars and trucks behind you are very noticeable by their headlights, and this particular truck's headlights were the brightest I had ever seen! That truck was also larger than any others. One of my grandpas was a trucker for a while for PIE in the Pomona area of California years before, so I have noticed a lot of trucks. This was a monster! How our little car was blocking the ramp and the trucks surrounding me didn't, I have no idea. So as I pull onto the highway and get up to speed, I noticed him behind me. I looked to my left as I merged onto the right lane, then on to the left lane to make room for him, but when I looked back in my rearview mirror, he was gone! Not pulled off, not jackknifed anywhere—gone! It was like he vanished from the planet! Even Steve looked for him and couldn't see hide nor hair of him anywhere. We got goose bumps!

Anyway, we decided to go on ahead to the next rest stop to sleep. We heard the next day on the radio that there was a loony that had stabbed some people to death at the very rest stop we had originally stopped at! Thank You, God, for Your mighty hand and protection! He promises in His word to protect us and be our rear guard and shield of protection to His children! His word is true, and His promises are yes and amen to us! Hallelujah!

> For He shall give His angels charge over
> thee, to keep thee in all thy ways.
> —Psalm 91:11 (KJV)

CHAPTER 3

Bikers, Pushers, and Witches

We lived with my family for a couple of months when we came back from Washington state and were able to get into a little two-bedroom apartment on Fort Lowell less than a mile from Steve's Taco Bell assistant manager job he found almost immediately upon arrival to Tucson.

One of our neighbors was a middle-aged woman from Turkey. She was lovely! She adored Mary. She came to Mary's first birthday party and had bought her a stuffed puppy. Mary carried that thing around for years! They were about as inseparable as you can get. As nice as she was and as cute as our second apartment was, we wanted something of our own. We started looking into buying a home.

We went through a realtor named Larry to find something, and he did! He found us this nice single-extra-wide mobile home that was for sale. It had been on the market over the whole summer, and still no buyer, so the price was reduced.

When we went to look at it, we fell in love with it. It was beautiful! *However*, the previous tenants had pets and, therefore, fleas. Those fleas were locked up in the home all summer with all windows shut and locked and electricity off—so no air-conditioning with the late summer Tucson heat and humidity—so they were everywhere! We walked into it, looked around, and then Steve looked down. Our legs were moving, but we were standing still, discussing the deal to buy. We were covered to the waist with fleas!

We went home immediately; and not having any other option, we both jumped straight into the little pool at our apartment—clothes, shoes, jean shorts, everything. Of course, we cleaned up our mess in the pool, but oh my goodness! We had fleas around even after treating our car, apartment carpet, and furnishings for a few weeks. We were able to talk the owner into replacing all the carpet in the mobile home and having it professionally treated in order for us to buy it, which he did and we did.

We were in our new home mid-November of 1988. In our purchase, we had them move it to a nice mobile home park at the Country Club Estates Mobile Home Park on Country Club near Ajo Way. At the writing of this, I am unable to find it on the map or bring it up on Google, but the Kino Sports Complex has been created and is near where I remember living, though my sister says it is still there.

I found a job as assistant manager of National Video at Golf Links and Kolb. That was a lot of fun and gave me free movie rentals, but the pay was minimal, and the hours were limited and usually during the only times we could spend together. My mom and/or one of my sisters would watch Mary during my shift, then I'd head over and take her sleepy little form and, as gently as possible, put her into her car seat, which would always inevitably wake her up. Frustrating, let me tell you.

One day, a prior coworker of Steve called him up and said he had left Church's Chicken and had bought the Dairy Queen on Alvernon over by the De Anza Drive-In Theatre. He and his wife were sole owners and needed help getting it going. He asked if we could help out. Well, Steve had to continue to work for his Taco Bell and part-time Church's Fried Chicken job on Grant Road to keep us above the drowning-in-bills line, but I could. The pay they offered was about what I was making at the video store, but the hours they needed me to cover were better hours for us as a family, so we agreed, and I gave my notice at the video store the next day.

God is so good. He knew that the video store was about to close down as "mega" video stores like Blockbuster was coming into the area and took almost all of the members/customers. I worked there for a few months, but when things didn't continue in a friendly manner or according to the verbal agreement we had made (but rather like Jacob and Laban in the Bible), Steve and I decided I would quit.

I found work at the nursing home on Grant Road called Devon Gables as a nursing assistant. This is 1988, before they had to be certified or known now as CNAs or PCTs (patient care technicians). I had taken the job because they had promised to certify me within six months, and that certification was going to be able to keep me employed just about anywhere and further my medical career. They didn't. Every time the class was scheduled, something would happen, and they would cancel it or postpone it. They never did have that class. While working there, we found out that we were pregnant again. Praise God!

They had me working in the Alzheimer's wing frequently as I knew the songs and movies that these residents talked about most of the time, and I had a lot of patience for them. While working there, my mood became darker and darker, and Steve, Mary, my mom, sisters, and friends did not like the depressed state I seemed to be slipping into. It broke my heart how so many of my patients (sorry, residents) were "thrown away" into that nursing home (and others) and forgotten. I would spend almost all of my breaks and lunches—and even come in and bring Mary with me on my days off—with some of the residents, especially those that had no other visitors ever that I knew of.

Oh the stories those residents could tell! Amazing! The Bible mentions in a few places how important listening to the elderly is. The lessons and pain that we could save ourselves from just by listening to the "wisdom of the aged" are too numerous to count. The main time many of them had any visitors at all was right around Christmas time. I guess the family wanted to stay somewhat in their elder family members' good graces, not to mention their wills.

Anyway, they would come and spend about five minutes talking with their "loved one" and then spend the rest of the hour they "bestowed" on them yelling at the staff for "stealing" their items. Most of which weren't stolen, but due to the acidity and frequency of their family members' incontinence, they were worn through and had to be discarded. If the residents were lucky, their family would bring one new package of undies, maybe a pack of socks, and two pairs of pants for the men or two to three snap-front gowns for the ladies and expect that to last for the whole year. The way so many treat the elders of their family drives me nuts with irritation! Sorry, I'm getting off track.

Anyway, while working in the Alzheimer's unit one day in January 1989, I was in a room, and the man thought I was trying to kidnap him, so he pulled his legs up and let them fly with all the force he could muster. Luckily, I saw it coming just before he connected with me and was able to turn my pregnant belly out of the impact zone. He landed on my right hip, but with enough strength that I started leaking amniotic fluid.

Boy, you have never seen nursing home staff move so fast! They had me in a wheelchair and halfway to the front unit and then plopped me into an available bed with what seemed like twenty pillows under my feet within minutes. They wouldn't let me move until the medical director checked me over and then only when my husband and mom came to get me. I was put on early maternity leave from that very day. Everything turned out okay; I just ended up with a very large bruise on my right hip, and of course I was very sore for a few days. Steve never let me go back when my maternity leave was over either.

While on maternity leave, our second child, still in the womb, kicked Steve out of bed in the middle of the night! We had a queen-size waterbed with leather-padded sides and drawers underneath. To just get out of that bed on one's own was a feat in and of itself, but when one is very pregnant, it's near impossible! When he landed on the floor, he was not happy to say the least! He yelled, "Ouch! What did you do that for? I would've got out without you kicking me!" To which I replied, as I held my belly tightly, that it wasn't me, the baby had done it, and I thought the baby had come out through my skin at the same time! He couldn't believe it till he saw the little foot do it again. Powerful even before birth!

We didn't know yet that the baby was going to be a girl. In fact, when I was pregnant with Mary, our first child, he wanted to find out, but I refused. We finally agreed that we'd find out for the second baby. Every time we went in to get an ultrasound during that pregnancy, however, she would twist her legs up and curl into a tight ball so no one could tell. The doctor said that this one was the most modest baby they had ever encountered. She still is, by the way!

Now at this point our finances were tight, and with me not working, they became extremely strapped and very dependent on the miracles and provision of God Almighty to meet the needs and pay our bills. As we prayed, we both felt that God was calling Steve into the Navy. The Navy? We live a few miles from the largest Air Force base in the country, and God is directing him into the Navy? We prayed and fasted; and the more time spent in prayer, the stronger we knew Steve was going into the Navy. So we set about seeing what was needed for him to do so. He went to the recruiter and was told he was a little older than most, but he was within their guidelines at twenty-eight. When they found out I was pregnant and expecting in March, they refused to allow him in until after I delivered the baby. They had all paperwork drawn up for signing, but put it away until he brought them the birth certificate.

You need to know that I was born on my dad's twenty-fifth birthday, March 10, 1969. My dad and I were very close till he died on October 31, 1986. Bethany was due the first part of March, so of course everyone was hoping for a third generation birthday baby for my dad's day—a third generation birthday date, so to speak.

On March 9, we started doing all kinds of things to get me to go into labor. True, I had dropped already and looked like I was going to be in labor any second, but nothing happened. My "adopted godparents" John C. and Liz came down from Phoenix to be there and help. I took cod-liver oil (*yuck*), did squats, and we started brisk walking farther than I had been to that point. I went to bed that night exhausted.

The next day, March 10, we went to the mall, a park, and they sent us (Steve and I) to "run to Dairy Queen for some ice cream and get back before it melts." It was like three blocks away—funny! Still no contractions or labor pains. On Saturday, Mar 11, we went to the largest swap meet in the country, the Tanque Verde Swap Meet, and walked—no, jogged—through that place multiple times in and out of every lane, around the exterior, crisscrossed the area, and up and down every aisle as fast as possible to get me to go into labor. Nothing! We finally gave up and played games at Mom's place, then went home to our trailer about 8:30 p.m., exhausted again, while Mom, John, and Liz stayed up talking and playing more games. They said a few days later that they had a feeling it was going to happen that night or in the early morning, so nobody wanted to go to bed.

I got in the shower after we got home; and while in the shower, I started feeling some pressure, like a tight gripping across my low belly, and my low back started aching. When it happened a couple of times, I asked Steve what time it was but to tell me what the *exact* time was. It was 9:11 at that point. Nothing else happened, so I got out, dried, got my nightie on, and dropped into bed. At 9:29, it happened again. *Great*, I thought, *eighteen minutes apart. I would go into labor when I'm already exhausted from trying to go into labor! Just great!*

I think I was asleep before I hit the pillow. Next thing I know, I feel like I'm being ripped wide open at the belly and, wow, was my low back screaming! It was 11:08 p.m. I tried to go back to sleep, but there it came again! This one had me sitting up. I looked at the clock; it was 11:11. Only three minutes apart! Well, I guess I said it out loud because Steve woke up, yelled, "Three minutes apart?" and literally jumped out of bed. I think he jumped directly into his clothes; he got dressed so fast! He was putting his shoes on in less than a minute after he had woken up.

He helped me up since we had the waterbed, and it was very difficult for me to get out of it at this stage in the pregnancy. He got my small suitcase, grabbed Mary and her bag of stuff, and loaded everything up the car. I called mom's house while Steve was getting Mary in her car seat, and it didn't finish the first ring before she answered! Mom said they had just gone to their rooms because they had a feeling it was going to happen tonight, so they were up and will be waiting for Mary where my sisters would watch her while all the adults came with us to the hospital. Steve made that twenty-minute drive in twelve minutes. I remember him taking a right turn. I looked back, and little Mary in her car seat was almost horizontal; he was going so fast. She was laughing and saying, "Wee, Daddy fun!" Telling him to slow down was not even heard; he was so worried about getting me to the hospital.

After getting me to the Tucson Medical Center, he seemed to settle down a bit once they wheeled me into a birthing suite. Unlike Mary's birth where I was in a room to labor then whisked to a delivery room then to a postpartum room, the birthing suite allowed me to be in labor and deliver all in one room. I was doing fine, but, oh man, those contractions! With Mary's birth, I had had an epidural; and as I was so sick, I remember almost nothing of her birth. So with this one, I was not going to have any meds so I can remember every little thing.

I never knew that your body can sometimes be your own worst enemy. After being in full labor for over seven excruciating hours, the doctor came in and said that I am still not fully effaced nor has my cervix completed to a "ten" even hours after they had broken my membranes. The doctor recommended I have an epidural due to the amount of pain and possibility that my labor can continue for many more hours. "What? How many more hours?" I could not possibly make it with this much pain for "many more hours!" I remember looking at the clock, and it was 7:30 a.m. I said, "Okay, I'll have the epidural."

They must have been waiting right outside the door as within a minute, they were completely set up in the room and ready to go. I was told with Mary, I had to have three tries as the first two missed. Well, with Bethany, I had to have three tries as the first two missed! Those were so very painful. Here I am in full labor, having contractions to rip me in half, and they want me in as tight of a "little ball" as I can get over my huge belly!

To top it off, while in said "little tight ball," I had to take a big breath (*hah!*) and hold it while they stuck this huge needle in between two vertebrae. They did it three times before they got the correct spot. My mom, Steve, and Mom T were there with me the whole time. Dad T was also there, but he chose to stay on the other side of the curtains once all the misery began. Can't blame him one bit!

After the epidural, my pains reduced drastically. Hallelujah! I was finally able to relax and try to rest between contractions. The doctor came in about 8:00 a.m. to check me; and miraculously, I was at a ten and fully effaced! I was so angry. I could have made it another thirty minutes of labor! I told the doctor so too, and the doctor said that if I hadn't gotten the epidural, I most likely would not be at this stage. My body was so tense that it was what was causing the barriers to getting where I needed to be. Come to find out, it's pretty common.

On Sunday, at 08:12 a.m., Bethany Joy Hall was born. She was nine pounds 10.5 ounces. She had dark curly hair, beautiful blue-green eyes like me, hair down her back, and chubby rolls everywhere. Everything was perfect. When they took her to the nursery to get cleaned up and all the stuff they had to do and check her over, which they said was going to take a while, they moved me to my postpartum room, and I was asleep within minutes. Steve stayed with me, and when I woke up, Mary was there. She loved the way my tummy moved in "waves" every time she poked it. She couldn't believe that my tummy was so small since she saw me last—only yesterday! She was so excited to hold her new baby sister! They were best friends from the moment I lay Bethany in her arms. Being only eighteen months and four days apart, people told me I had twins the hard way. I agree! We were able to go home on Tuesday, March 14.

When she was two weeks old, Steve was whisked away to the US Navy boot camp in San Diego, California. It was hard, but with Mom, all three of my sister's help, and God's strength, we did well. Steve enjoyed our letters, and he was able to call on occasion. I helped work in my mom's cleaning business. When he graduated boot camp, my sister Heather and I took the girls to see Daddy's graduation. They loved playing at the beach, and we tried burying each one in the soft, cool sand. They had so much fun! We stayed at a little cheap motel near the base. He was kind of excited that he had been told the 32nd Street Naval Base was going to be his station. After our weekend, he had to go back to the base and start his A school training, and the girls, Heather, and I went back home to Tucson.

After he was out of school, he stayed on his ship, the USS *Acadia*, which was a destroyer tender ship in a fleet. A tender is the "fix it, all supply, creator-of-fresh-from-salt-water, weapons vault" ship of the entire fleet. It is also the least able to defend itself. They only had rifles and handheld guns for defense, but they were also dead center of the fleet while out to sea, so anyone wanting to get to that ship had to go through the ring of ships and small patrol boats first. At the time of this writing, she has been decommissioned, which means she is no longer in service. The Navy has since gone with all nuclear powered vessels, and she wasn't one of those.

He had two friends aboard the ship that hung out together a lot, Brian and Larry. Brian had an apartment in El Cajon ("The Box" in Spanish), thirteen miles due east of San Diego, with his girlfriend at the time. He had Steve stay over quite often when they had days off together. Those three guys were pretty close for a long time. When Steve was on base on his days off, he and Larry would go to the base theater and video arcade. That theater had a lot of premiere movies, and more often than not, some of the actors would come to see the audience's reaction to the film. He met Mel Gibson, Steven Seagal, and many others by always sitting in the back section. One day, at the theater, he was sitting in the "lucky seat" and won a coffee mug that he was able to have any color and for it to say whatever he wanted printed on it. He chose a blue one and had them put "Melody, the Greatest Wife" on it in big bold black letters. When he brought it to me on his next trip to Tucson, I cried. That was midsummer 1989, and I have it still.

Once every other month, he would take a flight to Tucson, and we'd be able to spend thirty-six hours together before he'd have to fly back to San Diego, get a taxi, or literally run from the airport to the base to ensure he didn't get back on board the ship late. Those were wonderful weekends but bittersweet also. Knowing he was leaving after a day and a half was heart-wrenching, but to not see him at all was even worse! In the early summer of 1990, he found out that an apartment was opening up in the complex that Brian lived in, and it was affordable, even on an E-4's salary. We had the military move us over, which we never did again, and were finally able to resume being a full-time family together.

This place was, well, let's just say it was interesting and definitely kept you on your spiritual and physical toes! We were one apartment of only four in that entire complex that were not filled with drugs, drunken parties/bashes, or witchcraft paraphernalia. It seemed that everyone was either a Hells Angel" a drug pusher/producer/addict, or very active in a witch coven nearby that hated us.

When the managers evicted people, most of the time, the hazmat people would have to be called to clean out the apartment to make it safe enough to rent to someone else. One place was so bad, there were hypodermic needles sticking up all over the carpet in all the rooms to where one had to be wearing steel bottomed shoes to enter. This place was quite the place for colorful conversations. Our family became well-liked by most everyone there, and I became friends with the other three "clean" families, Brian and his girlfriend (of course), a woman Connie, and my soon-to-be best friend Virginia. During the few months we lived there, we were able to build relationships with all the families in the apartment complex.

This was the beginning of God's using us as a type of "fix it crew" for His body, the church. We found a church right away, a Church of God in Christ close by. It just so happened that the church had been praying for God to help them build their bus ministry. We helped to get it up and running at full blast in just a few short weeks. By the time we left that complex, every apartment but two had at least their kids, if not one or both parents, attending church on a regular basis. The manager hated it when we left; he said that since we had moved in, the crime and destruction had taken a huge decline there as well as in the area, and he just knew it was because of us. We even held some Bible studies and were known to help anyone if we possibly could.

God changed that place in a huge way. It was the difference from a moonless midnight to the noonday sun. He not only kept us very safe, but His love allowed everyone to love us and even become quite protective of us and receptive to Him and the Gospel of Jesus. The few that didn't, they either moved away or just accepted us as neighbors that they could depend on. Amazing! I remember thinking about this place when we first moved in, and it always seemed dark.

With the spiritual darkness that was there as well as surrounding it for a few miles, it is no wonder. When we left in September, it seemed a much brighter and much less "questionable" place to reside. All glory to God!

I'll never forget, at fifteen to sixteen months old, Bethany one day went missing. I couldn't find that girl anywhere, and half of the complex helped me search for her. She was found two doors down at Brian's place. She was up on a barstool eating a Filipino dish of soup made with bok choy, other veggies, and pork ribs served over rice; talking up a storm while shoving the food in her mouth with his girlfriend. She ended up making it a habit as his girlfriend was always home and cooking something. God is so good. He kept our kids safe even when they found ways to "disappear!"

> To give light to them that sit in darkness and in the shadow
> of death, to guide our feet into the way of peace.
> —Luke 1:17 (KJV)

CHAPTER 4

Rescue Me

*F*or Mary's third birthday in 1990, we went to Tucson for the Labor Day weekend to have her party with all of the family and my godfamily from Phoenix. We had a wonderful time; but as usual, the days flew by, and it was time to get back to El Cajon so Steve wouldn't be late onboard the ship the next morning.

We left Labor Day at about noon. It is only about an eight-hour drive, so we had plenty of time with a couple of hours to spare for him to hit the hay by 10:00. We got there about 8:30, and while he unloaded the stuff, I put the girls to bed and listened to the messages on the answering machine. Two of them were from his ship. They were calling everyone back to their station immediately, and if he wasn't aboard the ship and checked in by 22:00 (10:00 p.m.), he would be considered AWOL (absent without leave), and that meant big trouble. He had just over an hour to get to the ship.

He called a friend to find out what was happening and found out that their fleet was shipping out early in the morning, and all he knew was they were heading to the Persian Gulf. Steve hung up, and the first thing he said to me was that he was shipping out to the Persian Gulf, and if things went the way he thought they were going to go, he didn't want me to be stuck here in California alone with the girls during a war. I tried to convince him otherwise, but he would have none of it.

He called my mom, and to our surprise, my godparents were still there. We told everyone what was happening and that he wanted me to move home until he returned, but he couldn't be here to help me move. John and Liz called the parents of the child they were babysitting that weekend and asked if they would mind if they took the child with them to help us. They had no problem, and within the hour, they let us know, and they were on the road to my rescue.

Steve packed his duffel bag and literally ran to the trolley for the last trolley to the base that night; he barely made it. That was the quickest goodbye we ever said to each other! He said he checked in at 9:57 p.m. Praise God! We had informed the apartment manager, who was not happy, but completely understood and let us out of our lease with no penalty or fees of any kind. Bless his heart! God worked everything out perfectly, as usual!

I started packing things that I knew we would be taking with us to Tucson and packing other stuff to put into a storage room there in El Cajon. I think I finally passed out about 2:00 a.m. John and Liz pulled up to our apartment about 6:00 a.m. Poor Dad T. was looking really tired! I fixed them breakfast; and after we cleaned that up, we split up. Dad T. and I went to get boxes while Mom T. stayed with the little boy and our girls and got them packing their toys and clothes. We were out of the apartment, cleaned and everything early that afternoon.

The girls and I said goodbye to all our new friends and hit the road to our new home in Tucson. Mom put us in my old room, and we got creative with what stuff we brought with us. My sisters were happy to see us and have us home for good (at least for six months). Steve had been told they would return after six months. When he first went into the Navy, he was told he would never be gone more than six months at a time. Well, he was gone a bit longer; leave it to the military.

They got to the Persian Gulf in late October or early November that year. They were the one fleet that initiated "Desert Shield," and the fleet that served in the Desert Storm Gulf War that began January 17, 1991 at 2:55 a.m. Iraqi time, which was January 16, 1991 at 6:55 p.m. EST (USA), and a cessation of hostilities was declared on February 28, 1991 at 8:01 a.m. Iraqi (12:01 a.m. EST, USA). I tell you, I have never watched more television—news in particular—than I did that month!

I worked about every day, and I worked extra-long hours. If I worked an eighteen-hour day, I spent three of the remaining hours with the girls and three sleeping; if I worked a twenty-hour day, I had two hours with the girls and two hours to sleep; and so on. I have never agreed with people wearing headphones at work, even as the office/business cleaners; but during this time, I did. I was constantly watching, or at least listening, to the news for any tidbit of information of his fleet or even his ship.

The stuff that he saw and witnessed was unbelievable. So much senseless death and dying by Saddam Hussein! I found out later that one of my brothers-in-law Tim was in the Army 101st Airborne "Screaming Eagles" ground forces in Iraq. God kept them both safe! He kept us safe back in the States too, even from my lack of sleep.

I will tell you that those few months we were preparing for and at war for Operation Desert Shield/Storm were some of the longest days of my life. Though Steve wasn't here, God was; and every single day, He made His presence known. He calmed our fears and placed a warm blanket of His peace over each of us. My flesh rose up and was addicted to hearing any tidbit of news or coverage of Steve's battle group; my spirit-man *knew* that God was in control, and Steve was going to be okay through all of it. Thank God for His all-encompassing presence!

In those days, we didn't have cell phones, Snapchat, Twitter, or even Facebook. We had the old-school things like a regular landline phone at home; paper and pens for letters sent via the US Postal Service; packaging items for things like care packs from home full of homemade cookies, snacks, gum, books, cassettes of audio conversation, and on rare occasions, video tapes. We survived!

Steve would spend fifty dollars for a ten-minute phone card while on land in the Kuwait area, and then would have to stand in line for up to two hours in order to make that ten-minute phone call. Once, he and Larry squeezed into a little photo booth together that made a seven-minute video and sent it to me. Oh, wait, that was a different deployment! Sometimes, the deployments just run together.

He returned in May, and they were all given a couple of weeks off. We met the ship for its celebrated return. That was super cool seeing hundreds of sailors in their Dress Whites lining the edges of the ship as it slowly made its way into port and dock. There was no ticker tape parade, but they had all kinds of stuff all along the pier and throughout the entire base. The girls were enjoying the free ice cream and really couldn't care less about the big ship coming in.

When he came down the gangplank, I was so excited! My amazing husband was finally home, safe and sound! Praise God! That ice cream gave us a distraction for the girls so we could just be in each other's arms for a while. He actually had to stand in front of them for several minutes before Mary even noticed he was there. She jumped up and came running to him, jumping into his arms. She was so happy to have her daddy home! Bethany, on the other hand, glanced up and smiled, but nothing was taking her away from her ice cream. Remember, though, that she was two weeks old when he went into the Navy, and he had been gone for most of her life. It didn't take her long to remember who he was, though.

Of course, we were living in Tucson, where the girls and I were staying with Mom during that vacation. We drove straight there. His first night back, after we got the girls to sleep, we got ready for bed. I remember praying that he would be able to sleep through the night without having any nightmares of the war and some of the things that he had seen firsthand. So he hopped into bed and was asleep, I think, before he even hit the pillow, snoring loudly but looked very peaceful, so I didn't mind! I got into bed and started to cuddle next to him. I've been told it's called spooning.

Anyway, I scooted so I was next to him, but he immediately scooted back. I scooted back until I was next to him again; and once more, he scooted back immediately. Well, I wasn't to be deterred, so I scooted yet again, and this time, when Steve tried to scoot back, he realized he was on the very edge. So he put his arm down between us, sat up and yelled, "Who the heck are you?"

Granted it was dark, he was in very unusual surroundings, and it had been almost a year since we had been in the same bed together, but I was taken a bit off guard. It dawned on me that all of the time on the ship, he told me he had a few occasions where he had to, let's just say, "guard" being alone on his cot. I slowly rolled over onto my back, looked at him, and quietly said, "I'm Melody, your wife. I'm allowed to be here."

He sat there for a few minutes, letting that sink in, and then he touched my face, gave me a kiss, and said, "What? Oh, yeah. Sorry."

To this day, we laugh about it; and when something weird happens, one of us will pipe up and yell, "Who the heck are you?" We laughed about it that night after he remembered where he was. It was the only thing I've ever had to deal with, by the grace of God, regarding his absence from his family and being thrust in a war halfway around the world. God not only rescued me on a moment's notice and got our girls and me safely to Tucson, but He rescued Steve from having the evils of war stuck in his head and heart and brought us together again to glorify Him together!

> My brethren, count it all joy when ye fall into divers
> temptations; knowing this, that the trying of your faith
> worketh patience. But let patience have her perfect work,
> that ye may be perfect and entire, wanting nothing.
> —James 1:2–4 (KJV)

CHAPTER 5

Dying at Balboa Naval Hospital ER

*W*hile living in El Cajon the second time at the Bradley Gardens Apartments, we had friends throughout the complex. Many of those friends were military families. One of them was a newlywed couple, and I had basically adopted the wife as a kid-sister type. She loved having the girls over and spending time with us regularly. We'll call her Kim.

One afternoon, Kim called me with a big problem. She was bleeding—a lot. She was soaking through several Heavy Maxi Pads every hour and having severe cramps. They only had the one vehicle, and her husband had it with him, so she had no way of getting to the hospital. I told her I would take her shortly as I had to find a sitter for the girls. I called another of my friends (she was glad to take them), packed them over to her place, came back, and grabbed Kim. We put a trash bag on the seat topped with several towels, and off to Balboa Naval Hospital in San Diego we went. There was a saying back then about that place: "hurry up and wait, and wait, and wait, and wait!" There was a reason for that saying.

We got there in the midafternoon. When we got to the window/desk to register in, she told them why she was there when they asked. "Okay. Have a seat. We'll be with you shortly," is all they said.

She told them exactly how much she was bleeding, and they said, "Yes, ma'am, we understand. Have a seat. We'll get to you shortly."

Several hours later—it was two to three hours at least, and the waiting room was filling up with every passing minute—we were still in the waiting room. I had brought some cards and another game to play with her as well as a book and my Bible to read; knowing the reputation of long waits, I wasn't surprised. I was concerned, however, with the amount of blood loss she was experiencing, and we were still in the waiting room. I got up and asked the desk every half hour or so how much longer they think it would be and always got the same response: "We're seeing patients as fast and thoroughly as we can. Not much longer now. Please take a seat."

It really was difficult not to get frustrated. After playing a few card games, she pulled out her book and began to read. As I went to get mine out, my eyes were drawn to this young man who was just helped in by two guys in naval uniforms. They leaned him up against a wall as there were no more chairs, went and registered him in, said something to him, then patted him on the shoulder and left. There was something very wrong with this sailor. I heard the Lord say, "Go pray for that man for healing." I looked around at how many people were there, and I remembered several occasions where I had prayed for someone, and God didn't heal them; so if I prayed, and God didn't heal him, everyone would think God is dead, and/or I was weird, so I stayed in my seat. I didn't seem to remember the times that God *did* heal many people that I had prayed for. Isn't it interesting how the enemy seems to get our focus on us and the negatives? Pride is a huge faith and obedience killer!

This sailor was tall and pasty white. He seemed very sick. "Go pray for his healing." Still I sat, howbeit very anxious for him. His eyes were droopy; and frankly, he seemed like a wet noodle. He "slithered/withered" down the wall till he was on the floor. I jumped up to see about a wheelchair when a hospital staff member came out with one for him and helped him get into it.

"Go! Pray for him." I finally started over, and wouldn't you know it? They wheeled him to the back right then and there! Oh no! I've missed my last chance! I prayed for God to give me one more chance somehow, and I would pray for him. I prayed for God to forgive me for disobeying and for being fearful of men. I felt so ashamed for letting Him down and possibly allowing that poor man to suffer or die.

A little while later, Kim was called to the back. As we passed through the doors to the exam rooms, we passed right by that gentleman. I got my friend settled in her room and told her that I'd be right back. I then headed out to see that man and pray for him. I almost reached him when I heard two nurses talking about him. I slowed down to hear what they were saying and was horrified to learn that he had been bitten repeatedly by a brown recluse spider. "Had he gotten in here sooner, we might've been able to do something. So sad!"

He looked like death warmed over, and that is an exaggeration for the better, let me tell you! His heart rate was way too fast; his pupils were pinpoints and kept rolling back in his head; he was breathing rapid, shallow breaths; and his body was wet from excessive sweating. He was shivering and couldn't even keep his head up.

I went up to him, knelt down, and asked him if I could pray for him. I'll never forget hearing his very weak, barely whispered, "I wish somebody would!" I laid my hands on his shoulder and started praying. Now, one thing about me is I pray like my daddy prayed, very Pentecostal, full of gusto, and loaded with scripture. I took authority over that venom, commanded his body to be healed in Jesus's name, quoted some of my favorite "healing" scriptures (like Isaiah 53:5, 58:8; Jeremiah 30:17; 1 Peter 2:24; Psalm 103:3–5, 107:20; Malachi 4:2; and Exodus 15:26), told him that God loves him very much, hugged him, and told him that I was supposed to pray for him out in the waiting room, and I was so sorry that I didn't. I asked him to forgive me for not doing it when God told me to.

He forgave me; and as I stood to go back to Kim's room, he was no longer sweating, he had normal color in his face and arms, his heart rate was dropping down, and his eyes looked normal. He sat there looking like a perfectly healthy sailor. It was like watching the scene in *The Lord of the Rings: The Two Towers* when King Theodin was possessed, and Gandalf removed the hold over the king that Saruman had. Then you watched the wretched old out-of-his-mind shell of a man ready to die go through a very immediate metamorphosis into a much younger, stronger, healthier, and in-his-right-mind King Theodin—and all within minutes! It was absolutely miraculous!

The nurses and doctors who had been working on him were stunned! They started doing all kinds of tests and finally released him. They told him that they didn't understand how, but when he checked in, he was on his deathbed, and there was nothing they could do about it; and now, just a short while later, he was a completely healthy man. They couldn't explain it. He was a miracle.

Funny thing happened next too. When I got to my friend, she suddenly stopped having cramps and felt better. She also stopped bleeding within minutes of my coming into the room. God will use whatever He needs to in order to get His people where He wants them to do the purpose He has for them! After a little while and some tests on her, she was released. That sailor was waiting outside on a bench for someone to hitch a ride back to his ship with as the people who dropped him off were unreachable. Guess who gave him a ride to his ship? Ya betcha (that's Minnesotan, by the way) I did! I asked him how he got bitten by the brown recluse and asked what the doctors said; and after he answered my questions, I talked about the goodness of God.

To this day, I kick myself for not being obedient at the very beginning. What if I had been obedient, and he was miraculously healed right then and there in that waiting room with all one hundred people to witness it? How many more healings could've happened that evening? How many lives would've changed? How many souls would've been redirected from an eternity in hell? I wish I could tell you that I have always been quick to obey after that day, but I can't. I have failed miserably many times with the very same thing. I can tell you that I try to be quick to obey and try not to allow the fear of man to dictate my actions or nonaction. I can tell you that God still loves me and still uses me even after I fail Him. I can tell you that when I asked for forgiveness, He fully and completely forgave me and doesn't even remember it.

But I do, and the enemy knows I do. The devil tries to use it against me even now, more than twenty-five years later. Usually, I realize it and remind him that I've been forgiven, so go away and take those condemning thoughts with him; but there are those times that it gets in. I am so thankful for God's grace, mercy, and total forgiveness! He healed that man even after I refused to pray for him because of my pride. He healed him in spite of me and my disobedience. He healed him even though He only got glory from a few rather than many. Someday, I will meet that young man again, and I will also meet a few, maybe many, who were changed because of that night he was dying in the Balboa Naval Hospital ER!

> They shall take up serpents; and if they drink any
> deadly thing, it shall not hurt them; they shall lay
> hands on the sick, and they shall recover.
> —Mark 16:18 (KJV)

CHAPTER 6

Angels Unaware at McDonald's

*W*e went to Tucson and Phoenix quite regularly while we lived in El Cajon. It was only about an eight-hour drive, so we tried to go at least once a month. When we got to Yuma on the border of California and Arizona, we knew we were at the halfway point. There was a McDonald's at the junction of the I-8 and the I-8 business highways. We would stop there for a bathroom break; and if we had enough money, we'd buy a cheeseburger for a dollar each for the four of us, a large fry to share, and Steve would get his soda.

One time, we were really financially strapped and still made the trip. The kids had been sick for a while, the kids I babysat were sick, and I was getting sick and tired of being cooped up with them 24-7. We barely had gas money to get us there and back. I ended up finding six dollars in the bottom of my purse, so when we got to our regular Yuma McDonald's, we got five cheeseburgers and Steve's soda.

We were starving, and it was hot. I remember ordering six cups of water even though there was only four of us. When we pulled around after getting our order at the drive-through window, we noticed a homeless man sitting on the curb at the entrance/exit with everything he owned in a shopping cart he was leaning against. I felt this urging in my spirit to feed him and give him some water. I told Steve, so he pulled over next to the guy. I opened my window and said that I had a cheeseburger if he'd like it as well as some ice water. He was so grateful! He said that it was the first thing in a couple or three days that he's been given to eat, and he thanked us over and over again. I felt bad that the cheeseburger was all we had, but we were broke too.

I now know why we ordered the extra cheeseburger instead of any fries like we usually did; God had a plan! So we gave the gentleman his food and water and blessed him. We treated him with respect and dignity. The girls were so excited that we were feeding the man. Mary turned around in her seat to wave, but he was gone!

Now that intersection where the driveway to McDonald's was had clear vision for the entire parking lot, and we had just left him seconds ago. He was completely gone. He and his shopping cart had disappeared! The girls couldn't believe it! Was he a ghost?

God opened a door to teach a truth from His word that day. I told them that in God's Word, we are to treat all people like we would Jesus because we never know when we are talking with angels and not know it according to Hebrews 13:2. They talked about that encounter for years; and every time we went to that McDonald's, they reminded us of it and wondered if we'd ever see him or another angel.

God uses times like that to teach us that He is here, and He gives us opportunities to come alongside Him and join in what He is doing in our lives and the lives of those around us.

CHAPTER 7

God the Mechanic

*O*ne time before Daniel was born, when we were coming back from visiting my family and godfamily in Tucson and Phoenix, respectively, we were in our vehicle, and we suddenly started having engine trouble. Now, if you've never been on Interstate 8 from Arizona to San Diego, California, there is a dead zone for cell phones (not that there were many of those at this time [1991–1992]), traffic, towns, etc. I mean, there is nothing there or around for miles, and traffic is almost nonexistent, to say the least. So we stopped and checked all the fluids, tires, battery, cables, etc. looking to see if there was anything loose, empty, or generally not up to par. We found nothing unusual, so we got back on the road (from the shoulder) and continued on our way home.

Suddenly, the engine sounded like someone was hitting it with a hammer, and a bunch of alarms came on in the dashboard, and then it stalled and died right there in the middle of the highway. We were able to coast to the side of the road, thankfully, and of course there was no traffic in either direction to be seen. We were stuck, and we had no way of fixing anything or getting help.

We had just had a wonderful weekend and a wonderful service at church, East Tucson Church of God, with Pastor Larry Rice. It was a great service where the Holy Spirit showed up, and miracles happened. Lives were touched; hearts were changed; and when we left, we knew God was doing something mighty, as usual!

Our kids were getting a little antsy, and our time was ticking away before we had to be home. When you're in the Navy or any other branch of the military, they don't accept being broken down on the side of the road for an excuse for not being at your post. I looked at Steve, and we just seemed to know what we were each thinking.

We smiled and told the girls that God was going to fix our car. They weren't amazed at all. They expected Him to fix it! We told them to bow their heads and touch a part of the car—anywhere—as Steve and I put our hands on the dashboard. I started praying and said, "God, You alone are God. You can do all things but fail. There is nothing impossible or too hard for You. Father, You know we have to get home, and we have no money or means of fixing this car, and there is no one around to help but You and Your mighty angels. We pray right now that You would heal this car so it won't have any more issues all the way home or after that in Jesus's name! You said in Your Word that when two or three agree as touching anything, You would do it according to their word when we pray in faith believing. We are agreeing right now that this car is fixed right now in Jesus's name. Thank You, Jesus, for Your touch on this car and keeping us safe. Amen."

That was it. Short, sweet, and to-the-point kind of prayer, which I am *not* known for. Steve went out and shut the hood, got in the car, and started her right up! We never had another problem with that car all the way home or any other time that I can think of. God is so good and hears our cries. He wants to bless us and show His love on His children.

Another time, Mary was just learning to drive, and we were in our red Chevy Suburban on Interstate 80. That particular highway is known for being a trucker's highway. She was driving the leg of the trip we were taking and was going to switch out when we reached Ogallala, Nebraska.

Now, I have always liked being around truckers and have never had a cause to dislike them in general or individually. However, that particular day, I was sure close! The speed limit was seventy-five miles per hour in that area, and Mary was driving. She started to pass a truck, but when she came alongside it, it sped up and wouldn't let her pass. Then a truck ahead started slowing down, and a truck behind sped up, and they boxed her in.

She was scared out of her mind. She actually was crying and shaking and having a panic attack. There was nowhere for her to go, and they were forcing her to almost ninety miles per hour. The trucker in the back of us was so close, I could've opened the window and touched his front grill. She almost let go of the steering wheel; she was so scared. I was in the front passenger seat and started talking to her in a calm and gentle voice and telling her what to do, not to take her hands off the wheel, and then I started praying for God to intervene on her behalf on these truckers. In less than a minute after I prayed, the one next to us that she had originally tried to pass slowed way down and she was able to take that opportunity to get passed him and over. Praise God!

The next few miles were like God came in and swept away all the truckers. They just seemed to go away. Praise His name. She was able to finish her leg of the trip with no problems, and just a few miles away was our stop. She was so glad she was able to get out of the driver's seat that day!

Another time, there was a trip to Tennessee where Steve's parents and sisters lived. On the way home, we had no air-conditioning. We got into the canyons around the south part of Wisconsin when we had a blowout. It was so hot that the roads' heat about melted our tires and caused one to blow. It was on Interstate 90 between Beloit and Janesville. We had to unload everything in the trunk to get to the spare; and when Steve took the spare out, it was flat! We were stuck out in the middle of traffic on the shoulder of a very busy highway, on one of the hottest days in Wisconsin's history, with three adolescents/teenagers, and no spare or AC! We were praying and asked God to send help.

Just moments later, a trucker pulled up behind us, and after he got out and assessed the situation, he took Steve and the spare to the next town to get it fixed and brought him back. He didn't leave until he made sure we each had a bottle of water. They were gone about an hour, and when he dropped Steve off, he also dropped off more bottles of cold water. He even helped Steve change the tire and put all the stuff back in the trunk.

While the kids and I waited, we left our stuff next to the car away from traffic and found a patch of shade that we could all fit in. We weren't scared, just superhot! We all were beet red, and sweat was pouring down our faces, and even our clothes were soaked by the time the guys got back. After that, we were back on the road within about twenty minutes!

When we have no AC, we use the old "4-65" method of air conditioning: going sixty-five miles per hour with all four windows down! I ended up with heatstroke but was able to recover by the grace of God without any hospital/medical bills. God healed me.

From that point on, however, I was not able to be out in the sun when its rays were intense until Steve and I moved down to the Houston, Texas, area. Go figure! It was like I was allergic to the sun. Every time the sun hit my skin—period, at all, for any length of time, and no matter how small of an area the sun directly hit my skin—I would get an instant migraine, nausea, vomiting, and took hours to recover. The longer I stayed in the sun, the longer it took to recover. God moved us down to Texas, and I miraculously have no issues with the sun's touching my skin. Praise the Lord!

For with God nothing shall be impossible.
—Luke 1:37 (KJV)

CHAPTER 8

1994

From 1990 through 1995 we lived in El Cajon, California, which is about thirteen miles due East of San Diego, California. I had gone to the vo-tech in La Mesa, California, for phlebotomy and medical laboratory assistant certifications. I had graduated top of the class in both classes. I *loved* phlebotomy, drawing blood! In order to graduate, however, I had to do an internship. For phlebotomy, I interned at Balboa Naval Hospital, and then for the next course, medical laboratory assistant, I was blessed to have our personal family practice doctor, Dr. Leslie M. Morrisset, allow me to do the internship in his office. After my internship was completed, he offered me the job permanently. I gladly accepted, of course! He had no insurance benefits for his two employees, but we got free healthcare as far as doctor stuff, office stuff done as needed, including weekends and nights for the employees and our families.

Dr. Morrisset was one of the best diagnosticians I have ever seen. He would check his patients, ask some questions, and then order specific blood to test for things that are extremely rare. And when the results came back, he was absolutely right every single time! It was amazing!

He also had the old-school mentality of the barter system for some of the patients he cared for that couldn't afford to pay with money. He even made house calls for some. Many of his patients had been seeing him for three generations. He was a great man and cared for many things and people. Every year, he would go on his own medical mission in Haiti and other third world countries in South America, flying his own personal Cessna plane crammed full of medical supplies for his holding clinic there.

There was one time some of his patients had horses that needed to be exercised. They found out that I and my family loved dealing with horses and told us to feel free to come over and ride. We made plans to ride on Saturday, January 22, 1994. It was only a little over a week away, and the weather was supposed to be perfect! We were so excited!

Their daughter met us there and helped us saddle the pregnant mustang that Mary and Bethany were to ride together, but they had no saddle for me. I had no problem riding bareback, so I mounted my black Arabian quarter horse after putting the bridle on. They only had the three horses, so Steve would ride next and stay behind and watch Daniel, who was just over one year old. We followed her out the corral and down the old road that led to Mission Beach.

Now, I need to add at this point that the devil had been attacking our family almost daily with major problems to get us to lose our faith in God the Father. I absolutely loved being on horseback and, therefore, had let my guard down. About halfway to the beach, something—not a tremor/earthquake, snake, or noise but something I believe spiritual, even demonic—totally spooked the mustang on which the girls were riding. She reared a bit, nostrils flared, and did an about-face. She then took off at a panicked gallop with the girls holding on for dear life as they rode helter-skelter on the old asphalt road with chunks and giant potholes everywhere you looked.

I was able to maintain my horse and keep him under control. However, the young lady with us, her horse followed suit after the mustang and bolted straight for a road sign that flung its rider off and to the ground. It was like something out of the Road Runner/Wile E. Coyote cartoon with a sign that bends all the way to the ground behind it and then flinging Coyote flat onto his face directly in front of the sign instead of flying through the air to catch Road Runner way ahead as he had thought.

After I checked to make sure she was okay, I tried to catch my girls. With their horse at a panicked gallop and with a head start, I gave up, let go of the reins, and let my stallion go—and boy did he! I was gaining on the girls when I noticed Bethany slipping off the back toward the left. Mary was holding on tight as can be to the mare's mane, where her fingers were woven in, and the horse was starting to slow down. Bethany was thrown and landed on the side of the road into a giant cocklebur bush. She had cockleburs rolled into her underwear, shirt, and pants, and the burs were sunk deep into her skin.

I checked again, and Mary was sliding, but the horse was now at a regular gallop and still slowing down, so I got my horse as close to where Bethany was, and I slid off, landing hard on my left hip. I jumped up and ran to her and started cleaning her up as I picked her up. I then turned and noticed the mustang was riderless a ways ahead and started running to where Mary had fallen onto the road.

The young lady that was with us caught up with me then and took Bethany from my arms so I could get to Mary. There were two men walking along who had seen Mary fall off the horse; they ran to her rescue, helped her up, brushed her off, and then proceeded to yell at me for my horrible parenting skills. I thanked them for helping her and then took her with me as we started walking the rest of the way back to the stables.

She had a black eye, and we all had scrapes, scratches, bruises, and bumps. A few minutes later, as we limped along, a car pulled up whose driver had seen us heading to the beach and then saw the horses running home alone. She loaded us up and drove us to the stables where Steve had already started to put Daniel in his car seat and was coming to get us. He looked in relief mixed with horror at us as we emerged from the Good Samaritan's car. We called Dr. Morrisset, and after telling him what happened, he told us to meet him at the office for X-rays, exams, and cleanup.

We were hitting eighty to ninety miles per hour, hoping for a policeman. Never saw one, of course! We got there, and Mary's face was swollen on the right side, but she was having no typical signs or symptoms of any major issues like concussion. If you looked at her from her left side, she looked perfectly normal. If you saw her straight on, she was looking like a raccoon and swollen on the whole right side. After getting checked and finding no broken bones, we finished cleaning up our wounds, and he had me swear to keep him posted should Mary start to show any signs or symptoms. We limped into our apartment on Sunshine Road shortly after 2:00 p.m. The next morning January 23, which is my sister Heather's birthday, at about 7:00 a.m., Mary started vomiting. Uh-oh!

I called Dr. Morrisset, told him what was happening, and he said, "Well, get her to the hospital right now." I took Mary, and Steve stayed home with the other two kids. We went to Sharp Grossmont Hospital in La Mesa. The doctor there was horribly upset that we hadn't brought her in the previous day and started yelling at me, calling me all kinds of horrible names, and that I was a horrible mom, and he was going to make it his point in life to make sure she and any other kids I may have would be taken from me. He said if what was going on with her was what he suspected was really happening, he would be sending her via ambulance to La Jolla Children's Hospital.

So he sent her to get a CT scan, and while he was there with her, he wouldn't let me go with her. I called Steve. In tears, I told him what was going on and how this doctor was being so nasty and asked him to get a ride to join me immediately and have our neighbor Carrie watch the kids.

After we hung up, I called Dr. Morrisset and told him about this doctor and what was happening with Mary. Wow, was he angry! He hung up from me, called that hospital, and spoke to someone about Mary and me. He took care of that doctor to the point that he actually came and apologized to me later.

When that doctor came back with the CT results, Steve had just arrived. Noel, the manager of the apartments we lived at Sunshine Terrace had driven him to the hospital. The doctor confirmed that it was indeed an epidural hematoma; she had bleeding on the right side of the brain, and he was sending her to the children's hospital in La Jolla immediately.

While they were getting her ready to transport, I called our pastor at First Assembly of God of El Cajon on Pepper Drive Pastor Carl

Chitwood and his wife, Shirley (who was a RN), and spoke with him. It was during Sunday school, but he was in his office for some reason (*that* reason would be God). I told him what happened and what the doctor was saying and that Mary was in critical condition and was being rushed to the children's hospital via ambulance. He said not to worry, God's got this under control, prayed with me, and then we hung up.

I found out later on that he left his office, went to the adult Sunday school room, and said, "Excuse me, Ray. I need you to take over today and preach. Shirley and I are leaving right now to meet the Halls at La Jolla Children's Hospital. Mary is in critical condition, and may need brain surgery." Then he turned around, grabbed Shirley by the hand and left. You know what? They *beat* the ambulance to the children's hospital and were sitting in Mary's room, waiting on her when she arrived! I love those guys! That was an awesome church! It was the church I first preached in, but that was under an interim pastor prior to the Chitwoods.

Once we reached the hospital, right behind the ambulance, she was rushed to her room where she was met by her new doctor and our pastor and his wife. There, the doctor told us that the CT scan showed that her right artery had burst, but the amount of blood it was showing was not consistent with that kind of injury. Had that truly been the injury, she would have bled to death internally in her brain within a couple of minutes, not a couple of days.

The scans show that it looked like the bleeding had stopped, so he was going to wait till Monday morning, take fresh CT scans, and said, "We'll go from there. If the swelling and bleeding are down and stopped, we may be able to wait and see if the body will dissolve the blood that is present. If not, we would need to do surgery." Mary was kept comfortable, yet was not allowed to eat or drink anything at all due to the possibility of surgery.

First thing in the morning, she was taken to CT, and it showed that though it had greatly slowed down, she continued to bleed in her brain. It also showed an enormous amount of blood inside the brain area. The surgeon, who had been flown in from Colorado just for her, said that he recommends surgery at this point rather than waiting any longer. We agreed, and they started preparing her for brain surgery.

We told them that before they took her to surgery, we had to have a minute to pray with her, but the nurses seemed to blow us off. Next thing we know, they start wheeling her out the door. We stopped the nurse from taking her out of the room to surgery because we still had to pray with Mary. The nurse was really upset and was giving us a bunch of grief about it. I got bold and told her that the longer she lectured us, the longer it would take for us to start praying, which *would* happen before she could wheel Mary to surgery. She continued giving a lecture, and I finally interrupted her and told her to hush; we were going to pray now. She huffed but became silent. We all prayed with Mary, taking about two minutes, kissed her, and told her we loved her and that we'd be waiting for her when they got done. The nurse actually smiled and was nice from that point on. Weird!

Now at this point, I was still worried, but God had spoken to my heart that Mary was going to live. How much damage, I didn't know, but I knew that I knew that she was going to live through this. The surgery took several hours, and when it was over, a nurse asked us to go to this special room to talk with the surgeon.

When he came in the room, he was as white as his coat! He sat down and looked utterly shook to his core. He said, "I don't understand it, but I just finished a surgery on someone that should've been dead for two days! It went well, but she should've died moments after the accident happened." He told us how he had to cut a square of her skull out to get to the injury site and then described the damage done to her artery as looking like someone had stuffed a big firecracker into it and lit it.

The artery had burst and was shredded for several centimeters to the point that there was no saving that area of the artery. He had to dissect it, cut off the shredded ends, and connect the remaining ends of that artery together. He had removed a great deal of clotted blood and cleaned up what he could. Shirley asked if any gray matter had been damaged or lost, to which he answered no. Thank the Lord! He also felt that there would be no nerve or function loss, but we would have to wait and see for sure. She had sutures inside and outside of her head and was wrapped up pretty thickly, but he said her prognosis should be a wonderful and quick recovery considering the extent of the injury.

We thanked him for his hard work on our daughter and told him that God had His hand on this and had had His hand on him while he did the surgery. The doctor shook his head and said that he agreed wholeheartedly! That was the only explanation there was for what he had seen.

After she came out of the recovery room, she was brought to her room where we were all waiting. When she woke up, we all kissed her and told her we loved her and that she was going to be just fine. And then Pastor Carl and Shirley left. She went back to sleep of course, and we hit the phones to let everyone know how she was, what the doctor had said, as well as check on our other two kids. She was sitting up, doing her math homework the next day. For the next little over a year, she couldn't go outside without wearing a bike helmet. She wasn't allowed to do fast things like ride her bike, run, roller skate, or even jump on a trampoline for at least six months.

While she was there, I never left the hospital for any reason. Steve went home every day and went to work when he was scheduled, but I stayed with Mary. After she was out of the woods, my brother David came to visit and to try to take me out to eat to get some real food instead of the sandwiches from the hospital vending machine. When he got there, I told him I wasn't leaving the building—period! Finally, he realized I was serious, so he took me down to the cafeteria, which was closed, so we ate those sandwiches out of the machine anyway!

It was funny to me, but he was not a happy camper by any stretch of the imagination! He sat me down, gave me my sandwich and some chips he got us, and said he'd be right back with something to help pick me up. I had noticed a coffee cart that served things like lattes, etc. just outside the cafeteria and reminded him that I don't like coffee. He said I'd like what he'd bring back for me, he promised!

He brought me this Mocha Madness, which was *no* lie! I still remember the name of the drink, and I remember the fact that I *did* like it! I couldn't taste any coffee but lots of chocolate and chocolate whipped cream with chocolate drizzle and chipped bits of chocolate. Did I mention that it had a *lot* of chocolate? I loved it! Up until that point, I had only had two cups of coffee and liked only one of them! That was Yuban on a plane en route to the *We The People 200* in Philadelphia, Pennsylvania, in July 1987, just after my high school graduation. I was part of the Palo Verde Concert Choir, which won the opportunity to represent the state of Arizona for the huge celebration over the Fourth of July. Anyway, I have been a "coffee fiend" ever since!

That poor family that owned the horses were so very worried. They were worried for our health and welfare, but knowing what kind of world this is, they were sure we were going to sue them. We had told the daughter at the stable when we were loading up the kids and taking them to see Dr. Morrisset right after the accident that we were not mad at them, it wasn't their fault, and not to worry about it. Stuff happens, and we had let our guard down, so the devil had an opportunity, which he of course took full advantage of!

Well, just before Easter, the mom had called me and said that her family would like to do something special for Easter for us. I tried to convince her she had no need, but she would have none of it. She said her family "adopts" a family every Easter; and this year, they had chosen our family. I finally agreed, and she was thrilled!

At Easter, the kids each got a beautiful handmade quilt that folds up into a pillow, dinner for the family, some games, and some other odds and ends. It was wonderful and gave them a chance to finally relax over whether we were going to sue them or not. I think it was a form of closure and an opportunity for God to reach out and show His grace and for them to finally accept the fact that we were true to our word and weren't going to sue them.

Mary and our family were able to be a huge testimony of God's grace, mercy, and miraculous power! We were able to minister to all the staff and visitors at that hospital for the short time we were there. Our horseback riding accident was on Saturday, January 22; Mary had surgery on Monday, the twenty-fourth of January and came home Friday afternoon that same week. God is so good all the time; and all the time, God is good!

This was January 1994.

In the first part of June, Steve came home from his job working for the Navy Housing Development, and he could hardly move. He was in so much pain! I asked him what had happened at work that caused this problem, and he told me that he had fallen off the ladder, getting out of a big hole they had been digging for the housing project they were doing. He landed flat on his back. He said it caused an old injury he got while in the Navy on the *Acadia* to act up with a vengeance. Just peachy! It took me a while, but I finally convinced him that he had to go to the ER at Sharp Grossmont Hospital.

They took him back for an X-ray, and it showed that he had an inflamed cyst that was wrapped around his spine just above the tailbone area, and the pressure from the inflammation was causing the pain, numbness, and tingling that he was experiencing from his mid-back all the way down to his toes!

Steve was lying on his stomach on a gurney, and I was next to him, rubbing his back where I could without causing any more pain, when the doctor came in and said that there were two options he could offer. The first was that he could take a large needle and stick him repeatedly with lidocaine for numbing it up then taking a scalpel and lancing the cyst, which would release the pressure that was causing all of his pain.

The second option was a bit more gruesome, but a lot less painful. He said that he would have some orderlies come and help me hold Steve down, and he would just use the scalpel to lance the cyst and release the pressure so that Steve would only have one poke—

and one poke only—instead of about a dozen that he would feel and a few that he wouldn't feel much doing the other option. Well, when he put it that way, Steve would only feel the one, which was by far the better option. Steve doesn't do well with pain, so just one doozy and done sounded the better way to go.

The doctor figured we would choose that one and had these two big orderlies (they looked like giant bouncers) each take a leg and had me lay on top of Steve across his upper back and shoulders and grip onto the legs of the gurney. He got between all of us and said on the count of three, we were to grip for all we're worth and to absolutely *not* let Steve move. Wow! No pressure there! Don't let him move or this procedure can cause him to be paralyzed or lose nerve endings or worse! I was scared, let me tell you!

Well, we all got into position, and then the doctor started his countdown. "One." I gripped those metal legs with all my might, praying from my depths. "Two." Those two bouncer-like orderlies braced themselves. "Three." The doctor stabbed that scalpel in, and the three of us holding Steve down were airborne! My husband is quite strong, and his legs are like solid oak trees. Those oaks lifted those guys almost two feet off the ground and almost got me off of his shoulders. The only reason I stayed where I needed to be was because I was clinging for dear life to those metal legs!

We were sent home with instructions to keep it clean, keep the area shaved if needed, and he was to take Epsom salts baths two to three times every day for a few days up to a week. He was to apply ice and was told absolutely no lifting or going up/down stairs or ladders. The doctor gave him an antibiotic, a pain, and an anti-inflammatory medication prescription as well as a work restriction note for his work. It was nice having him home, but he is not one that enjoys downtime very much. After the second day, he was pretty much climbing the walls! When he was finally able to return to work, he was ecstatic and went back with great enthusiasm, let me tell you!

November 1. Bethany and Daniel went to the babysitter's apartment, as usual, as I left for work and dropped Mary off at school while Steve was already at work. It was a decent day at work, and things were going on like a typical day at Dr. Morrisset's office when

I received this unbelievable phone call. Carrie was on the other line half sobbing and screaming with kids screaming in the background. All I was able to fully understand was that Daniel had ripped one of his fingers off! I got most of the important information that I could from her, told Dr Morrisset what was going on, and asked if I could go get him and bring him back, to which he immediately gave his blessing.

She knew we didn't have any health insurance, so she didn't want to call the ambulance at 911, so she called me to come get him right away. I think I got to her place in less than ten minutes and ran down the sidewalk to her apartment. You were able to hear him screaming all the way into the parking lot. Bethany was crying, saying that it was her fault, and Carrie had Daniel in her arms with what used to be a white washcloth wrapped around his right hand.

I quickly assessed the situation and knew I would not be able to handle him while driving to the doctor's office by myself. I took control and told Carrie's brother to please watch Bethany; and if she didn't want to go to school, she didn't have to go as she was way too upset. I told Carrie to come with me and hold him while I drove to the office. I plopped them in the front seat and strapped them in together and then ran around and jumped in and sped off. I bet you I made it to the clinic in less than five minutes. I didn't hit even one red light, which is unheard of, and, well, yes, I *was* speeding a little.

We got into the clinic and rushed into the open room waiting for us. Dr. Morrisset came in and carefully inspected it. The tip of his ring finger was literally dangling by less than a thread of skin. He said that, yes, he could fix it, but it would look different and not as smooth as it could should I go to the hospital. I asked him if this were his child, what would he do, and he, without hesitation, said he'd go to the hospital. Off we went! I pulled into the hospital at El Cajon General where Becky, my soon-to-be sister-in-law, worked.

I rushed everyone into the ER. After I registered, we waited and waited. Finally, as the washcloth was drying up, I asked for some wet gauze to keep his finger and the top third that was barely hanging on moist to help with possible reattachment when the nurse took us to a hallway, scolded me for that idea, and yanked off the blood-filled washcloth—none too gently, I might add—and wrapped it with dry gauze. I was not a nurse at that time but knew from paying attention and working with a wonderful doctor that she was wrong, so I did what anyone else would've done. I *gently* removed those dry gauze pads and found some saline-filled syringes that I soaked clean gauze with and reapplied the wet gauze to his hand.

He wasn't screaming too much now, but Carrie looked like she was going to faint; she was so upset. I had her sit down and do some breathing exercises. Now that she was calmed down, I also was able to get the whole story of what happened from her. She had an old hospital metal frame that held a bag for linens, which she used for drying laundry outdoors instead of hanging on a clothesline since clotheslines weren't allowed at the apartment complex. Daniel was being potty trained, and she had his washed training pants draped on it to dry when he and Bethany started arguing over the thing. Well, he was pulling it one way, and Bethany started pulling it the other. His finger got caught in the locking latch, and then he tripped backward and fell just as Bethany pulled hard the other way, and his finger tore off in the process. Daniel and I did our best to comfort Carrie. Accidents happen. She couldn't keep her eyes on every kid every minute of the day.

As she held Daniel for a little while, I used the public phone to call my best friend Becky. Becky was the hospital's quality assurance person. The QA person is who keeps the doctor's hospital policies as current and following the best known practice. The staff of a medical facility usually hops to attention when a QA person drops by. I told her where we were and how long we had been there, which really irritated her. She said she'd be down in just a minute and get things moving.

What I didn't know is that as soon as she hung up, she called a plastic surgeon who just happened to specialize in hands and who owed her a favor. She got downstairs to the ER within a few minutes, and when she walked toward me and we hugged, boy, you should have seen the hustle and bustle. We were instantly moved to a room that wasn't available moments before, and staff just kind of hovered nearby, almost falling over each other trying to help my son and me.

Then Dr. J. Otero walked in, and things moved seemingly at the speed of light! He looked at Daniel's finger and praised me for my quick thinking in keeping it moist; that just might have made reattachment possible! I couldn't help it, but yes, I did look at the nurse who had just a while before scolded me for doing it. She wouldn't make eye contact and ended up leaving the room. He asked about any allergies, and since I was comfort nursing Daniel, he told me I would be holding and nursing Daniel while he performed the surgery. I asked Carrie to call and inform Steve and to check on Bethany and ask her brother to please walk up and get Mary from school when she got out.

We were escorted into the operating room of the ER. I was told to lay on the gurney, and then they placed my little twenty-three-month old child into a papoose and only kept his right arm out. They then placed him in my arms and had me start nursing him. So there I was, lying on a table with my son and about seven or eight other people, men and women, and I had to bare myself to nurse him! Embarrassing! As it was absolutely necessary, and they all were medical professionals, I got over it pretty quick.

Of course, being inches from this surgeon reattaching Daniel's little finger with these binocular-type goggles that were on his head with super bright light pinpointed at the site, I became quite engrossed with the procedure; that is, until Daniel felt the needle and clamped down! *Ouch*! Once the lidocaine took effect, though, it was pretty smooth sailing.

Do you know, Dr. Otero didn't charge me a dime? Even after the postoperative checkups, he told me not to worry about it. He was sorry it happened, and he was sorry that he couldn't control whether the hospital would charge me or not. Remember, we had no insurance for this type of thing. I had a free doctor and medical care, but not surgeries, post-op checkups, ER visits, or supplies and medicines. Then Becky was able to get the hospital to cut the cost they charged us to almost nothing. They blessed us so much! Praise God! He provided for *all* our needs!

I tell you one thing, 1994 was *not* a good year, to be sure! *But*, it was a year that God was able to frequently really move miraculously in our lives and in the lives around us!

And we know that all things work together for good to them that love God, to them who are the called according to His purpose.
—Romans 8:28 (KJV)

CHAPTER 9

Wanted!

*D*ue to the specific content of this situation, some details will not be shared.

In 1995, we were feeling that God was getting us ready to move. We prayed about it and prayed about it and felt that we were to move back to Washington state. One of Steve's brothers worked at a tire shop, and his boss was hiring for a position at another branch. He worked it out for Steve to get the job, but he had to be there in April. Our girls were still in school, and I didn't want to pull them out. Plus, there was nowhere for us to live when we first got up there, so we decided that Steve would go up, work, start getting some paychecks, and find us a place to live. To save money, the kids and I moved into my best friend Virginia's apartment with her two kids. That was to be for six weeks.

One day, during the week before Mother's Day, Child Protective Services called me and said they were coming over. That is *never* a good phone call to receive. As a Christian mom in Southern California, I had heard of many occasions where kids are taken out of their homes because of the family's beliefs. Naturally, not all of them were true, but in this day and age, it only takes one. She would be there upon the arrival of the girls after school that afternoon.

True to her word, she pulled up within ten minutes of the girls' getting home. She came in and told me the situation (accusation) and then wanted to take my kids outside alone to talk to them. "Uh, no, they aren't leaving through that door with you, ma'am. You can talk to them in here just fine," I replied.

I had a really bad feeling about this woman, and my spirit was screaming, "Do not let them leave your sight!" She spoke with them and then told me one thing about kids, turned to my friend and told her the exact opposite! No kidding. Exactly opposite of what she told me, she was telling my friend about kids. I asked her about it right then and there, and boy did she get mad. Oofdah! She stormed out of that apartment in a huff. I knew this whole can of worms wasn't done.

After the kids went to bed, Virginia and I started on a plan. We were already planning on moving in a couple more weeks, so it was probably best if we left that week instead. I certainly did not want to cause trouble for her and her kids. So between the two of us, we had friends in almost every state in the country. We called every state and talked to them for exactly the same length of time. We figured that by doing this, no one would be able to figure out exactly where we are going. Some of the calls were to give specific information so that Steve would be made aware of the situation and the plan. We would leave California and head up to Washington, going through Arizona, Nevada, Oregon, and into Washington.

In southern California, kids can take up to two days every quarter or semester (I can't remember which) for "mental health days." Our kids hadn't taken any during the whole year at that point, so with all of the hubbub that woman created in the home, I told the kids they weren't going to school in the morning, and we'd discuss the situation tomorrow after a good night of sleep.

The next morning, I got up and called the school informing them of their taking a mental health day. The secretary told me I had to bring them to school; they couldn't miss. I informed her that by law, they were entitled to a couple of mental health days that haven't been utilized yet, so they were not coming. She argued with me for a few minutes until I firmly reiterated, "They are not going to school today. I'm sorry, but that's the way it is." Then I hung up.

About two minutes later, the phone rang. It was a friend of ours that works in the school office. She told me to get the kids and leave the apartment right this minute; the cops and that CPS woman from yesterday were leaving the school to come get my kids. They had been waiting in the office for the kids to arrive at school to take them into CPS custody, and when I called and told them they weren't going to go to school, the woman was furious! I grabbed everything I could possibly grab in about two minutes, put the kids in the car with the stuff, and took off to who knew where.

Virginia would be moving to Washington later that summer or fall and would bring our stuff from the storage unit we had rented with her, so we would get our stuff up there then. As we disappeared around the curve of Bradley Avenue, the police and the CPS lady came around the other end, so thank God we missed each other. God protected us so much! When they got to Virginia's apartment, she was able to truthfully say that we weren't there, and she had no idea where we were or where we were going.

We were able to park inside a garage at another friend's house and lay low that day. I was absolutely distraught that whole day! I had never been in trouble with the law, and now I'm wanted! I was being hunted like a criminal! Well, that very night, Steve got a message to us that really threw a wrench in the works. He was flying in to help me drive and deal with the kids. He was flying into the San Diego airport the next afternoon! I was planning on leaving the state by noon the next day, and now I had to wait hours before I could leave the state just to go to the airport to get him. *Ugh!* I was so frustrated.

My brother and I played spy games as kids (all through childhood and through the teen years as well), and we were quite good at it, and going to an airport when you are wanted by the law was *not* a good idea! That is one of the first places they lock down and flood with your picture and description. Let's not forget that I also had to wrangle all three kids at that airport with law enforcement searching just for us! That next day was going to be very interesting. I was sick to my stomach all night long just thinking of it.

Just remember, back in 1995, e-mail was not an everyday-and-everybody thing, nor were cell phones. We stayed at my friend's house for as long as possible the next day, then had to leave and find a place to wait until Steve's flight was due to arrive. We went to a Jack in the

Box near the freeway (easy access to escape if needed). We got a soda and small fries so we could sit inside and at a table that could see every entrance, but not be seen as easily.

Everywhere we went, I had the kids sitting on the floor of the car with our stuff around them, praying the entire time that we wouldn't be in an accident and get hurt. We arrived at the airport, and I found a parking spot halfway to the front by the entrance. I didn't want to be on either end because I knew those areas are especially looked at when police and security are looking for someone.

We got out separately, and I had the girls kind of walk near as if they were with a family or couple that could've passed as their own at a glance, and Daniel and I held back to not seem to be with them. I had all the kids go by their middle names, and the girls were to keep an eye on me and listen for my whistle. If they heard that whistle, they were to turn around, find an adult going toward the parking lot, and head back to the car. I saw Steve coming down the escalator, and after we made eye contact, turned Daniel and me around as I let out my loud whistle for the girls.

They were perfect! They kind of joined up with families that had kids that were of same hair color and were talking excitedly and the girls joined in their conversations. We walked at a brisk pace to our spot in the parking lot, and all jumped into the car. We made it out of the airport safely and never passed any kind of security or police. Talk about the grace of God in action!

Immediately after we left the airport, we went to my hospital job at National City Hospital to explain to my boss that I had to quit effective immediately and why, as well as to figure out a way to get my final check. Mrs. Villanueva was so shocked and angry at the system for this whole situation and worked with me to get my last check. From there, we went to bid farewell and get necessary things for us from Dr. Morrisset's office. He had all of our medical records gathered together, over-the-counter meds that we may need while we were summarily on the run, as well as my final check with a small bonus to help us out. He shook Steve's hand, patted the kids on their heads, and we were off. Bless their hearts! Both of my bosses and I cried. That was the last time I saw either of them.

Steve had filled up the car with gasoline, checked all the fluids, and made sure the tires had the correct pressures while I was at the hospital in National City, so we were able to drive to El Centro before we even thought about stopping. I actually begged him not to even stop there. "Let's wait until we're across the border into Arizona."

But he said, "No, we have both been up for the last two days, and we are getting a room for the night here. We will get a fresh start early in the morning. We are both tired, grumpy, and so are the kids. We'll get to Arizona tomorrow."

Nothing I said would swerve him from what I considered a foolish decision. Well, we stopped and got a room, but I hardly slept a wink all night. Every sound outside was, in my mind, the police and CPS finding us and surrounding the building, and they were going to crash through the door any second and take the kids away and put both of us in jail for trying to cross the border.

We were on the road before 6:00 a.m., safe and sound and together. Once we crossed the border, I felt like this humongous weight lifted from off of my shoulders, and I literally took a big breath in relief. That night in Nevada, I slept like a baby! I didn't want to risk going to any of my family or friends for a few days at least, so Tucson and Phoenix were both out of the question. I didn't want them to get into any kind of trouble.

Since we both felt that we were no longer in any (or much) danger, we made the remainder of the trip like a vacation. We stopped at historical markers, took lots of pictures at every place that looked cool or memorable. We lived on the McDonald's Dollar Menu and Walmart giant sub sandwiches.

We arrived at one of my brothers-in-law's place in Roy, Washington, neighboring Fort Lewis army military base a few days later. We had followed the Lewis and Clark Expedition trail for the last part of our journey. We kind of felt like those explorers of old as we left everything we had known up to this point and were off on a grand adventure, seeing new things, and going to new places.

We found out about six months later that we had actually been on the news as "wanted for questioning," and that I was on Southern California's most wanted list for a while. The woman who worked for the CPS had created such a fuss for finding us that authorities became suspicious of her and, after an investigation was conducted, found that she had had a personal vendetta against Christians and had made it her personal goal in life to remove, "save" every child that was under the care of parents who were believers in Christ Jesus, and put the parents in prison.

Once the authorities found all this out, they dropped all issues with me and our kids, fired her, took her into custody, filed charges for the illegal stuff she had been doing, as well as reopened all the cases she had ever worked on where kids were taken from their homes and families. She had destroyed so many lives; it was appalling! Some kids and their parents from our kids' school in El Cajon had seen our pictures on the news several times and kept up the information.

The Bible says that "vengeance is Mine, says the Lord. I will repay." In other places He says that He will bring justice, and truth *will* prevail. God is not a man that He should lie. What He says, He will do—period! Thank God He had His mighty hand on us throughout this entire ordeal.

CHAPTER 10

Lost!

Our First Day in Minnesota

We moved to Bemidji, Minnesota, in May of 1999. We had lost our house in Lacey, Washington, due to Steve's having an accident at work. Being injured on the job gave his supervisor Bill the opportunity he had been looking for to fire Steve. The owner of Holroyd's Sand and Gravel loved Steve, so Bill waited until the owner and his wife were incommunicado on the open seas. I remember Steve and I had felt that God was about to do something new in our lives.

One morning, Steve was very excited and happier than he'd been in a long time, especially since he was getting ready to go to work. We were doing okay financially. We were both working and homeschooling the girls. We had Daniel in a Christian school for kindergarten and first grade. We were running this huge food ministry in our area and the Nisqually Reservation nearby. We had big trucks leaving day-old items in our yard and then picking up items that were about to meet or exceed their "freshest by" dates, including milk, eggs, yogurt, cheese, sour cream, cottage cheese, not to mention the produce. I was well known as "the Bag Lady" because I *always* had a bag of food with me to give away to people.

Anyway, Steve went to work, and I did the regular routine with the kids. I worked morning and evening as a home caregiver for a young man that went to our church, Yelm Prairie Christian Center in Yelm, Washington. Michael had been born with birth defects and cerebral palsy due to his mom's doing drugs and smoking during her pregnancy. After his birth, his grandmother Norma adopted him as her own son. We adopted her as a grandma figure for our kids as their real grandmothers were many states away. Mine was in Tucson, Arizona, and Steve's was in Bemidji, Minnesota.

So I was taking my daily nap so I could work that night when Steve came home. He never got off that early. He came into our room and said in a very cheerful voice, "Honey, I'm home! I got fired today. God has amazing plans for us!" To which I promptly burst into tears. Fired? Are you serious? And he seems so happy about it! What in the world are we going to do without his income? How are we ever going to pay our bills? He gave me a hug, told me not to worry about it, that God had told him when he was doing his devotions that very morning that He was about to do something and Steve would be at His beck and call, ready and able to do work for the Lord Himself, and that he would be able to be available at all times. Well, having no job certainly made Steve available.

That food ministry fed us for a long time, let me tell you! I worked more hours and got another job for the daytime between the times I was to be at Norma and Michael's house helping him. God had Steve going to help elderly ladies, couples, people with handicaps, veterans, you name it. God told him to go to this person's house, or that building, or go down this street, and He told him what tools to take with him. He met a lot of needs for many people in our church, community, area, and family.

God provided for our basic needs, but not in our finances. It was so difficult to see this as God's will, but He really showed Himself faithful. We had a very good friend that told me that she had a very long conversation with God about us and how His Word said that if we don't work, we don't eat (2 Thessalonians 3:10) and the man that doesn't provide for his family, he is worse than an unbeliever and has denied the faith (1 Timothy 5:8). She was absolutely sure that we were *not* in God's perfect will for us, and she had to do something to get us back on the right track.

This is a true friend! Someone who, rather than downing their friend, take it to God and intercede for them for that situation.

However, God took her through the entire Bible, starting in Genesis, showing her many instances that He had His chosen people/person doing things and relying on Him completely, yet many thought the same thing about them that she did about us. He then told her she needed to apologize to us and bring us several bags of groceries of things that we didn't get through our food ministry. She was there the very next day! We cried together for a long time and spent some real quality time together. She brought us meat, beans, rice, canned goods, even some ice cream! Bless her heart! I sure miss Tammy!

After about a year, we were foreclosed on by the loan company and had to move. We had to be out of the house by the day after Mother's Day. Mother's Day again? I was really starting to dislike Mother's Day weekends. We loaded the largest U-Haul made with their pickup truck full vehicle transport, and the truck we had on it was loaded to the brim. We were ready to go first thing Monday morning. Steve, Daniel, and our dog Waddles were in the U-Haul, and the girls and I followed behind in our car, which was also completely loaded. Yes, we had a *lot* of stuff.

We stopped overnight just outside Bozman, Montana, that night. Steve had to use the restroom in the truck stop but locked the door to the cab as Daniel was asleep on the seat. The girls and I were asleep in the car parked right next to them. Steve came back, but couldn't get in the truck cab, nor could he wake up Daniel to unlock the door. After pounding on the door window for about five solid minutes, he finally woke up but couldn't figure out how to open the door. It was a *very long* half hour as we got him to roll down the window so Steve could get the door unlocked and open. It was quite an ordeal in the middle of the wee hours at a truck stop loaded with truckers trying to sleep!

Did I mention that it got extremely cold? Well, it got extremely cold! We all ended up in the car piled on top of one another for warmth and the few thin blankets we had on top of the pile. Waddles, our completely black Golden Labrador/German shepherd dog was even in the mix! A trucker who worked for a moving company saw the problem and came over with some of the extra furniture pads that he just gave us. He offered for us to sleep inside the cargo part of his truck, but of course, we declined graciously. So he gave us several of these super thick, quilted, furniture pads that were the size of a full-size bed quilt, and I would even say they were thicker than the average bed quilt. They were so warm! We ended up too warm before too long.

We arrived the next night at our new home. Steve's dad and mom, Milton and Rose, gave us their little two-bedroom, one-bathroom house out in Sugar Bush Township in Eastern Bemidji, Minnesota. It was twenty-three miles east of the town of Bemidji on top of a hill, and its backyard ended up at one of the many lakes. We had driven all day and through the night when we arrived in downpouring rain, and the roads were absolutely sopping wet. The ditches were brimming over with water, and you sank when you stood on any of the dirt for any length of time. Come to find out, Northern Minnesota was in a record-breaking rainfall spring. They had already had more rain that spring than they usually get in several springs put together, and it was still raining.

We decided to leave the truck at the end of our mile-long driveway at the top of the horseshoe access road and all loaded into the car to get to the house. We would attempt the driveway the next day while it was light outside rather than at night while it was dark and raining cats and dogs. We got to the house without any more fuss, grabbed the stuff we needed for the night and showers in the morning, and slept that first night in our new place on the floor. We were so tired! We all and the dog slept in the living room but couldn't find the switch to turn on any power. We used our flashlights and decided to just go to sleep and deal with everything else in the morning.

We got up in the morning and figured out where the power box was and the water well. After we got everything turned on, we set everyone to work, cleaning the place up and getting ready to get our big truck down the driveway and unload it. We went to truck and just about fainted. The truck had sunk into the mud road we had left it on all the way past the axles! Just the top half or so of the tires were visible. The big U-Haul as well as the trailer hauling our pickup were both buried! We decided to unload our pickup and use that to get help from town. We told the kids to stay in the house, finish their chores, and we would be back shortly. We had to get help to unload and get our big truck out of the mud.

When we tried to get the pickup off the trailer, we found another problem: the straps had worked their way under the springs of the frame of the truck body and wouldn't come out. We were going to have to cut the straps, but we had to have permission as it was U-Haul's property, though it was their fault they slipped under the frame.

We went to the U-Haul place we were to return the truck to and explained the situation. I had all the paperwork that proved the manager of the U-Haul we rented from had been the one to place the straps where they were, which allowed them to slip under the frame springs, so this manager on the receiving end had to approve us to cut the straps without our being charged for anything. We got home, got the truck off the trailer, and drove it to the house. We planned on unloading it and then unloading the U-Haul until it was light enough to get it out of the muck and mire. That was the plan, but we knew it would take all of us to get it done while it was still light.

We pulled up to the house and found it super quiet. No noise, talking, barking—nothing. We searched the whole house and yard; it had a big yard. No one was around. It actually looked like what I imagined it would look like when the rapture happened: vacuum on but flat on the ground where whoever was using it let go of it; a half-eaten bowl of cereal where the spoon had been dropped even with cereal still in it onto the table, missing the bowl; and a rag dripping off the counter by the sink where it was being soaked and dropped before it was wrung out. No matter how loud we yelled, we had no answering bellow. Where could they have gone?

Being new to the area, actually just hours in the state itself, we were so scared. What kind of area are we in? What kind of people are around us? Were there wild animals to be concerned about nearby? The only people we knew were our neighbors Frank and Lila, but they were on vacation for a couple more weeks. We had to get help and fast! We drove back toward town when I remembered seeing a sign from someone "official" nearby. We pulled into that yard, and I was out of the car before Steve even had it in park, running to their front door. They were the fire marshal for that area; and though they didn't have anything to do with search and rescue, they did have a radio to those authorities and were able to get a search party, the county posse for such times, on the move to our place.

They followed us home, and within an hour, we had met almost every one of our neighbors in a three-mile radius. Some were in trucks, four-wheelers, and even on horseback. I think we had four squad cars in and around our house. There were maps out and people breaking off into small groups taking this section and that section. We have never prayed so hard in our lives! One of the sheriff deputies drove his car down the county road that continued past our place on the grass and over a few hills.

Suddenly the radio squealed. "Were two girls, a boy, and black dog the ones missing?" came across loud and clear. *Yes!* They were found! Praise God for His amazing mercy!

"Affirmative," the woman deputy reported.

"Well, they're less than a half mile from their home. I will bring them in."

I about fainted. I was so relieved! Steve, on the other hand, was on the warpath. He started marching in the direction that deputy had gone to meet them. Boy was he angry! He was relieved, yes, but so angry at the "what could have been" that he was seeing red. The deputy saw him coming and told the kids to stay behind him, and he would talk to their dad. He reminded Steve, "All's well that ends well, and the kids were just getting to know the area. Don't be too hard on them. They had had a scary experience as well."

Steve thanked him for all he had done and for getting all the help out there to find our kids. He appreciated it all, but he was going to take our kids home himself and give them a spanking they would not soon forget.

As they all came over the last hill just past our house, the woman deputy saw his face, turned to me, and said she was glad they were found and that they were home safe. She needed to get all her deputies out of there. "And by the way, welcome to the area! You're going to love it here!"

Welcome indeed! We were in the state less than twelve hours and were already well known to the community. As everyone was leaving, many mentioned the giant truck buried in the mud at the end of the driveway. They all turned their focus on getting that truck out as their next neighborly project. They tried everything. Big 4×4 trucks, about a dozen guys pushing while a big truck pulled, people trying to dig out the mud from around the tires, everything anyone could think of was attempted, but to no avail. That truck hardly moved an inch.

One of our new neighbors, a Mennonite named Jed, said he would be back with "Big Bertha." "She'll get you out of that muck." As it turned out, Big Bertha was a huge tractor. It's tires were taller than me! He chained our U-Haul to her and told us, "Put the truck in drive and gun it when I give the signal."

Steve gunned it at his signal, and the dozen guys and I pushed with all our might, and Big Bertha pulled. She pulled about ten seconds when you heard this loud sucking noise as the mud released its grip on the wheels and axles! She got that truck out of the pit it was in! Hallelujah! Praise the Lord our truck was free at last! They all got our truck to more solid ground, and some of them stayed to help unload the truck. We were even supplied with dinner for a couple of days from that Mennonite family. Bless every one of those wonderful people! We had no words worthy of what our new neighbors meant to us from that first day in Minnesota!

So after we had a chance to settle down and talk to the kids about what had happened and why they had left the house, we were able to get the whole story. It seemed that Waddles had gone exploring and had come across a deer nest with a few does and a big buck. The buck didn't take kindly to our dog's nosing their nest, so he chased her away and right past the windows of our house. When the kids saw the big buck chasing their beloved Waddles with his many horns, they went into protection mode to save their dog and took off after the buck. By the time the chase was ended, they were several miles and a few small rivers and creeks away from our house with no clue how to get home.

One of the things we had been doing the entire time in Washington was teaching the kids survival techniques and what to do in the woods, wilderness, etc. We are told in the Bible that someday, being a Christian was going to make us live off the grid and in hiding, so we wanted the kids to know how to live off the land and stay safe. They did many of the things they had been taught and would have made it home alone if that deputy hadn't driven ahead and seen them coming.

At one point, they had written a note (our oldest daughter, Mary, was always writing and kept paper in her backpack, which she took everywhere she went), which they tied around Waddles's neck with Daniel's shoestrings and told her, "Go home and get help!" just like in the old *Lassie* TV shows. She looked at them like they had to be kidding, and there was not a chance she was leaving them alone, which she didn't until they were all home. They were so excited that they had done what they had been taught, and that it worked! They couldn't believe it! They had found their way home all by themselves!

We were well-known in the area from that time on, to say the least! God was so good and kept our kids safe. We all slept soundly that night.

> I will instruct thee and teach thee in the way which
> thou shalt go: I will guide thee with mine eye.
> —Psalms 32:8 (KJV)

> And in the wilderness, where thou has seen how that the
> Lord thy God bare thee, as a man doth bear his son, in all
> the way that ye went, until ye came into this place.
> —Deuteronomy 1:31 (KJV)

CHAPTER 11

You're Moving to Houston, Texas

*W*hen God tells you He wants you to do something, it is truly in your best interest to just say, "Yes, Sir!" and do it. Trust me, it's so much easier, and things can get done so much faster if you do! God has a plan for each of our lives, and whether we know it or believe it or not is totally irrelevant! He not only has a plan for us, He has a plan for our *good*, to prosper us and give us a future and a hope (Jeremiah 29:11)!

I became a traveling dialysis nurse for a travel dialysis staff company called Fortus Group in late 2015. My first contract was at a clinic in Kingwood, Texas, for US Renal Care starting January 18, 2016. Within just a few days that first week, Bernadette, the boss of the clinic asked me to take the permanent job that I was filling in for as I was a perfect fit! "We all love you, and the patients adore you! Please stay with us. The atmosphere is better when you're here. I truly don't believe in coincidence, and God brought you to us for a reason." She asked me and said those things almost every single week.

Now, I must let you know that prior to this contract, Steve had been struggling with his walk with God. He had been so active in churches every time God moved us to one, and after being so—well, I'll just call it what it was—abused and attacked, he started to slack off his obedience. Once you start going downhill with your faith, it isn't long when you are *way* down that hill before you know it! So he was rarely involved at our church in Bemidji, the Evangelical

Covenant Church, wouldn't hardly listen to Christian radio, read a Bible, or truly spend time in prayer.

Now, I'm not saying I was perfect, but I hadn't backed off my serving the Lord, and that in itself caused problems at home. It's hard enough to submit to one another, but when the other is not serving God, it's downright close to impossible! We don't fight often, but the arguments about putting God first were becoming more and more frequent! Once we got to Houston, we attended a church less than twelve hours upon our arriving, and Steve fell in love with it and with God all over again! It was miraculous! The look on his face when the pastor preached and a word from God was given and how the pastor responded to it was fabulous! He told me when we barely set foot in the foyer before we went into the service, "Honey, this is our church. We're home! We'll be going to this church the whole time God has us here in Texas!" What joy those few simple words brought to my heart!

It was a wonderful service, and we were late to it, so we didn't even get to sample their style of praise and worship! The clincher, I think, was when the pastor gave this blessing over the offering that he called "the tithers blessing" at the end of the service. *Wow!* I had to tape it on my phone like three times to make sure I heard every word correctly. I've been in church all my life and have *never* heard anything like it.

Most churches have a prayer over the offering, and then the ushers pass plates, bags, buckets, or whatever and collect tithes, offerings, etc. from the congregation while someone sings or music plays. Not here! No! The pastor says, "Let's celebrate what the Lord has done as we bring our tithes and offerings to Him." Then he starts saying this amazing blessing over his congregation while they get up and take their moneys up to buckets, or ushers bring buckets around if you are upstairs in the mezzanine, and people stand as he blesses something that touches or resounds in their hearts. There is cheering, applause, shouts of joy, and great enthusiasm during what I had usually seen portrayed as duty by the congregations.

We made that church, Crossroads Fellowship on East Sam Houston Parkway N, our home for the time we have been in

Houston. Since we've been going there, Steve has rededicated his life and has not just walked with God but has been *running* after God! It has been awesome!

We were in Houston, Texas, from January 16, 2016 to mid-March when I was given another offer for a permanent position at US Renal Care in Kingwood. Not just any everyday job offer, no! This was a once-in-a-lifetime kind of offer! Really good rate of pay, wonderful benefits package, ability to have the entire months of November and December of that year off so I could be in Minnesota with our middle child Bethany as she gives birth to her fourth child and for the first six to eight weeks after she gave birth, and several other perks. It was absolutely a golden opportunity!

Now, the question was, was this offer from God? Was it His blessing and His way of telling us, "You're moving to Houston"? Or was this an attempt from the enemy of our souls trying to sway us and get us out of the perfect will of God Almighty? We did not want to assume this amazing job offer was God's plan for us to move, so we had many people in many states praying for God to bring confirmation to us, but we didn't tell them anything about what we needed direction for.

We know how stubborn and blind we can be, so we had people praying that He would make it obvious. That means for us to move, well, that means we have to leave our family *way* up north, all three of our kids, our son-in-law Frank, Bethany's husband, Daniel's wife Hannah, then Mary's fiancé Scott, as well as the three amazing grandsons Jeremiah, Gabriel, and Elias, and with a grandchild on the way. What a difficult decision to make! I will admit that this was the one move I fought God on, and I fought Him *hard!* As with Abraham, sometimes God asks us to put our family on the altar of sacrifice. I cried a lot! I still cry, and we've been down here over three years so far!

That same week that I was given this amazing offer, I also got an e-mail from Joan Hunter Ministries saying that she's going to be conducting an ordination program that upcoming April! The amount it cost was *exactly* what we had left after paying all our bills for the month with money that we have *no* idea how it got into our account.

Back when we moved to Bemidji, Minnesota for the second time, I had gone to a healing revival at Tenstrike Community Church in Tenstrike, Minnesota. Guess who's healing revival? Yes, Joan Hunter's! God told me to go to it and get involved in the prayer team, so I did. On the last evening, God told me that I would be ordained through this ministry. Ordained? Me? Well, okey dokey then!

However, every single time I attempted to get any of the paperwork and red tape done, it kept hitting a brick wall—every time in every situation! How can I get ordained if I couldn't get the requirements done, letters written, stuff sent in? Lo and behold, I get notified that the nursing college accepted me that month and classes start in August that very summer! I couldn't be in two places at once, so I did the nursing program and graduated in less than three years with high honors, president of the student body, exquisite references, and winner of the State of Minnesota Community College Academic Team for Northwest Technical College.

Well, spring forward almost exactly six years later from my getting accepted into the nursing program, and I am a traveling dialysis nurse in Houston, and Joan Hunter Ministries is a mere thirty-five miles from our hotel door in Tomball, Texas. Who knew? A bunch of bills had to be paid, and I only had a little money left over. God is so good! Not only did I have *exactly* the amount of money I needed to take the course, I had every hoop done, sent in, and finalized within a week of finding out about it. It was like dominoes all lined up perfectly and everything falling into place smooth as silk! In order to become ordained through her ministry, I had to read about seven or eight books; listen to some DVDs; write reviews and testimonies; and pray, pray, pray, etc.

Now, when someone is obedient to God, you *know* the devil is not a happy camper! We got hit hard with all kinds of issues. We were being flooded with car problems, gas issues, illness—you name it! We were actually excited every time we got bad news! Granted, it was a roller coaster of ecstatic joy, then frustrated panic (we are human, after all), then right back to the joy! We knew in our heart that God would provide the means to meet all the situations happening, and that they would *all* turn out for our good. He healed our car; and to top it off, just because He could, He put AC in it! May not sound like a big deal, but let me tell you, when in Texas, AC is a very, very *big* deal! The car issues ended up being quoted at $2,300 and ended up costing a grand total of $189 with a rental for the three days we needed one thrown in by His grace with no cost to us! Praise His holy name!

On Thursday, April 7, I went to work and walked into a very high-tension situation. Two of the staff didn't like me and were saying that I didn't help people. In my thirty years plus of working, I have never ever been accused of that. I was very hurt and angry, I'll admit it. I told them both that not only was that not true, but I have helped both of them repeatedly ever since I got down there in January. They said I hadn't, so I got in the flesh and started telling them specifics of how I had helped each of them particularly.

Through the whole day, my stomach hurt. With each passing minute, it hurt worse and worse. It hurt so badly by the time I got off, I called my mom and other prayer warriors to have them pray. I even opted to eat a Cup-a-Soup for lunch to try to give my stomach a break. I thought it was due to all the tension.

Well, when Steve picked me up after work, he was ready to take me to the hospital. I told him to just take me to the hotel and let me take a nap before we do the ministry for CMA at Cycle Gear for April. On the way home, I called the Joan Hunter Ministries prayer line, and Sugar prayed for me. By the time I got to the hotel, the pain was gone, but I was exhausted. After a nap for about an hour, it was time to get up and go to Cycle Gear. I started to get the pain back just before it ended, so we ended up leaving by 7:45.

I was doing everything I could think of to relieve the pain. Through the day, I used a hot bag of saline to roll on my stomach and abdomen, took ibuprofen, and when we got home after Cycle Gear's Bike Night, I took as hot a shower as I could stand and went to bed with a hot pad. After tossing and turning and getting up and down, Steve had had enough! He said, "That's it! Get up and get dressed. We're going to the hospital. We were out the door in about ten minutes. I contacted the facility administrator of the clinic I was working at the next morning and informed her of what was going on.

We arrived at the ER at about 10:20 p.m., and it was a very, very busy ER. I finally got to the triage nurse about 11:30 p.m. They had a physician's assistant taking care of the patients waiting, so we were able to have tests, scans, IVs started, with results waiting by the time we got a room. They got an IV started, took blood for tests, and got a CT scan scheduled with and without contrast (a dye that is put into blood vessels that clearly show any leaks or blockages in them). That finally happened about 1:30 a.m.

I finally got a room in the emergency department at about 2:30 a.m. I had a male nurse, and he was wonderful. He made me as comfortable as possible and brought the doctor as soon as he came to the area I was in. After they saw me, poked and prodded me, asked questions, and listened to me with the stethoscope, they left to see if the CT scan results were read yet. Within minutes, they came barging into my room, hitting the door so hard, I thought it was going to come off its hinges! The doctor asked if I'd been in an accident. I said, "No," so he asked if I was being hurt at home, at which time they both glared at Steve. Steve looked at me, and we both had incredulous looks on our faces while exclaiming, "No!" They said they were keeping me for observation and possible surgery.

I ended up admitted to the hospital at Memorial Hermann Northeast in Humble, Texas (pronounced "umble," no H sound, by the way). I was admitted because my left kidney looked like it was in a boxing match and was taken, held, and punched repeatedly until it was a bloody, mangled mess. I had a sack of blood surrounding it, and there had been so much internal bleeding that my pelvis was full of blood.

They still cannot figure out why or even how it stopped bleeding. One of the things that had them baffled was the fact that though I had lost a severe amount of blood internally, my blood tests (known in the medical field as hemoglobin and hematocrit) showed that I was only slightly lower than the normal acceptable range. I didn't need a transfusion or a boost of fluids—nothing.

While there the next day, I actually asked God to send me someone who did not know me and vice versa to talk with me and, during the conversation, tell me His will for the particular situation of whether or not we were to move to the Houston area. And then, to really make it a "Gideon's fleece," I want that person to back it up with scripture!

Before I was discharged midafternoon on Saturday, April 9, I was walking around my floor and passed a little elderly lady that was in for a leg issue. God said, "Go in and pray for her."

I went into her room with her permission and asked if there was something she'd like for me to pray for her about. She said, "Well, I guess my leg!" indicating her wounded leg.

I gingerly laid my hands on it and prayed a simple prayer with her and her husband watching. When I got done, I told her to thank Jesus and wished them both a blessed day and walked back to my room. Next thing I know, nurses were running down the hall to her room. God had healed her leg! Hallelujah! He still works miracles today!

Sometimes, God puts us in places for specific reasons that have absolutely nothing to do with us, but He allows whatever to get us into the exact place at the exact time He wills it. I wasn't in the hospital because of me or any health issue; it was so I could be there and be walking down that specific hallway, passing that child of God's door at just that minute!

Wednesday night, April 13, finally came, and the ordination course/conference was underway! Day 2 was amazing, and just before the two o'clock session was to begin, I was filling up my water bottle with a very slow water dispenser when a tall black Nigerian man came up to me. His name was Praise! We chatted for a few minutes, and then he looked at me with a funny look on his face and said, "You are supposed to move here. You are supposed to move here to Houston area soon!" And then he proceeded to give scripture and verse as to examples in the Bible, specifically starting with Joshua and Caleb where God took His people up mountains, through forests, into valleys, up and down hills, and into their promised land where they prospered and bloomed mightily for Him and drew many to Him. I kind of looked up and grinned at God. I guess we *are* moving to Houston!

As the conference was about to resume, we arrived in the conference area and went to our seats (his was in the far back left section, and mine was near the front on the right), and the next session started. Charity Bradshaw was the speaker, and guess what her text from the Bible was. You guessed it! She wanted to tell us about two of her favorite people in the Bible, Joshua and Caleb, and how God sent them up mountains, through forests, into valleys, up and down hills...you get the idea. She used the very same verses and stories from the Bible that Praise had used and in the same order!

I started laughing. I looked up toward heaven and said, "Yes, Lord, I hear You! I know we are moving to Houston! Lord, You are telling Bethany [our daughter]. I'm not!" He did. On Friday, the next day, I texted the boss of the clinic and told her I accepted the job offer to which she responded with a new and very improved offer that I accepted. It was as if God was waiting to see if we would be obedient and move before really showing me my true job offer that is such a mighty blessing! Then to top it off, I received my ordination on Saturday evening at 7:00 p.m., April 16, 2016.

Monday, April 18, 2016, the "tax day flood" hit Houston. The area we lived in, Greenspoint, was one of the hardest hit, but I was going to go to work. Steve said the only way he'd let me go is if he drives me there, to which I replied, "Then you need to get dressed. We need to leave in five minutes."

We went through water higher than the floor of our car, and as we went through it, I noticed we both lifted our feet up just in case water came in. I knew God had a plan because our little car was able to get through some deep areas; and just as we passed them, police barricaded them and closed down the freeway behind us. I was the only nurse that made it into work that day, thankfully as there were several patients at the clinic waiting to be let in and out of the pouring rain. Steve stayed with me, and I had him manning the phones, which were ringing off the hook!

I went around, making sure everyone was safe, warm, and had something to drink as we were going to be there a long while, and then making phone calls to all other patients, telling them to stay home and remind them of our emergency plan. We only did a handful of treatments that day as a PCT (patient care technician) finally was able to come in about noon, and then my boss had to put us up in a hotel as I couldn't get out of the Kingwood area to get back to the hotel we were staying at.

That week, work was a madhouse! Schedules were crazy and rearranged, flooded-out patients as well as flooded-out staff; it was a mess! By Friday, I was absolutely exhausted. Steve had actually worked all that week at KFC in Kingwood as well. I got off at about 7:00 p.m. and was given a ride to his work so I could pick up the car. When I opened the door to go in and get the keys, I heard audibly, "Go to Minnesota and get a vehicle. You have the next four days off."

Wow. What a good idea. Crazy and pushing the limits, but a great idea. Steve really needed to have a vehicle since my hours are weird, and I still do on-call shifts for DaVita Dialysis in various areas like Cleveland, Conroe, Magnolia, Huntsville, and College Station, Texas. I asked to see Steve for a second so I could get the keys. He came out and asked what I was planning on doing with my four days off, and I said, "I'm going to Minnesota and driving a vehicle back here."

He looked at me and said, "Wow, that's a great idea!"

He gave me the keys and went to finish his paperwork and was talking with his boss. She asked him what I had planned, and he told her. She looked at him and said, "Well, you can have the next four days off. Just call me Monday and let me know how and where you are. You're done now. You may as well punch out and go home now."

He couldn't believe it! At 8:00 p.m., I booked two one-way flights to Fargo, North Dakota, leaving at 9:30 the next morning. We paid about six hundred dollars for them both together. We took the SuperShuttle to the airport, and everything just fell into place. We somehow managed to get VIP tickets, so we didn't have to remove shoes or anything else. We were practically ushered through the security post and were the first from our flight to arrive at our gate.

The entire trip up to Fargo was awesome! Instead of having to take a taxi to the mall where Hannah (our daughter-in-law) worked, she had been sent home due to having too many staff at work. She got off just in time to pick us up at the airport minutes after our arrival! We went to their apartment and left moments later to meet with Daniel at a nearby Taco Bell for lunch where he told us it would probably be late before he got off. We went back to their place, and a couple of hours later, he called and said he was off already and on his way home. He got home about 5:30 p.m., showered, changed, loaded an outfit for each of them, grabbed their dirty laundry to do at our place, and we left for Bemidji, Minnesota. We arrived about 8:20 p.m.

Sunday morning, we were able to be at church even before the family arrived and got attacked by the three grandsons when they got there. They hugged us so tight! They were like little love leeches clinging to me with all their might. I really cried. I was going to have to tell them that God wanted Mamaw and Poppa down in Houston, far, far away. I was not looking forward to that conversation. After church, I went with Bethany and the little boys to the store and bought her a Caribou Coffee before I told them the news of our moving to Texas. She said that the boys took it this time much better than when she and Frank told them a while back. They already knew? They didn't want us to move away, but if God wanted us there, then we had to go. What amazing boys that are growing up to be mighty men of God!

We spent the day with them, packed a few things into duffel bags and boxes to bring with us down to Houston, and Steve and the guys (Daniel and Frank) helped load the motorcycle into the pickup truck's back end and strap it down. We spent time playing games and having dinner at Frank and Bethany's with all the family that night. We had a sleepover with the older grandsons Jeremiah and Gabriel at our house, and everyone met at Raphael's Bakery & Café the next early morning. We were on the road to come back to Houston by 10:45 a.m.

We stopped way north of Kansas City that night at 10:00 p.m. When we got back into our truck at 3:30 a.m., it was raining. From that point all the way through Kansas City, it poured and stormed and hailed almost golf-ball-sized hail and gusting winds! We prayed over everything in, on, and around the truck. We checked the radar, and it showed the same stuff for our entire trip home along the exact path we had planned to go. I looked up and prayed, "Father, we are being obedient moving down to Houston, we pay tithes, and are faithful in everything You've given us. That bike is a tool that You have given us to reach the lost. We cannot drive through this kind of stuff the entire way home. I want our path cleared a *lot* and much less wind, in Jesus' Name!"

In less than an hour, above us were very light grey clouds and in some areas, actually clear blue skies. But if you looked out either the passenger or the drivers' window, you saw very nasty skies, lightning, and rain pouring down. It barely sprinkled on us, and the wind was at least cut in half the entire rest of the way home. Hours after we arrived home and Steve unloaded the truck from all but the bike, while we were sleeping, it started raining and storming. God is so very good!

One more tidbit about this God-planned trip: while we were driving through Western Arkansas, we just happened to drive right past the front gate of the CMA headquarters! We couldn't believe it! Being a part of the Christian Motorcyclists Association was a lifelong dream of Steve's; and of course, we had to turn around, go in, and take pictures of us there! It was like going to a famous national site or monument. We were in absolute awe! The few people we met were super nice and helpful. They showed us around a little and took pictures of us before we left for the remainder of the journey to our new home. What an added blessing and just because He can!

The next step for us was finding a place to live. After looking and looking in person, online, in papers, asking others, our friend Ara introduced us to a friend of hers who was a realtor. She took us to several places, including a beautiful apartment complex, which is where we finally signed the lease to rent an apartment at the Marquis at Kingwood. It was a beautiful one-plus bedroom ("plus" means it's more like a study that has a closing door at the front but attaches to the master bedroom by French doors that don't have locking handles) with brand-new carpet, new upgraded ceiling fans and AC, granite counter tops, and black and stainless steel appliances. It even had a washer and dryer! We ended up paying more than we had expected to, but we cut our gas usage to almost nothing. We both worked about five minutes from the apartment, and we no longer had to use a Laundromat or washateria (as they call them down here in Texas) to do laundry.

The move-in date was the last day of my contract with US Renal Care for Fortus Group. As of the next Monday, May 30, I was an official employee of US Renal Care. What a whirlwind we have been in! That seems to be how God works most of the time in our lives. We get a "memo," and after confirmation happens, *boom*, everything moves really fast! It's exciting and yet a bit scary all rolled into one big, giant rapidly moving snowball going down a very steep hill with no resistance!

After my accepting the offer was made known, boy, things started to change! You remember what I had said about the devil not being a happy camper? Well, he was livid and used everything and everyone it seemed to try to get us to change our minds. The first couple of weeks of May, both of us started having issues with staff at work—I mean bad can't-work-like-this type of issues. It got so bad at my clinic that some of the patients even asked what was going on, and one of the staff, a new believer, came up to me and said, "I'm so sorry that this stuff is going on. I have no idea what caused it, but you certainly don't deserve to be treated this way. What is being done is very unprofessional and downright mean and nasty! I am so sorry that you have to go through this garbage!"

I thanked her and felt such a relief! I know that sounds weird, but I had actually started to think I was being paranoid and going a little crazy! What affirmation can do! When she confirmed that it was being done and others could and did see it, I felt much better. It's hard to explain, but her doing that made me feel that it was not just in my head, and I knew God was going to take care of it.

He did! Once I realized it wasn't in my head, I gave it over to Him, and He completely intervened. I know my Redeemer lives! He gives me strength to carry on and fulfill what He has purposed for me to do. I've had many patients actually ask me to specifically pray for them for various issues, especially healings. God has been faithful and has done all I've prayed and asked Him to do. I've had patients that are believers tell me that they have been praying for me, especially when they see what the enemy is trying to do to get me out of there. It's a wonderful thing to be able to pray at work with others without fear of reprimand and allow the patients to pray! The opportunities here to minister and grow are astounding. Yes, my heart is and will forever be in Minnesota as long as those kids/grandkids are there, but I am glad we moved to Houston!

> And Jesus answered and said, Verily I say unto you, There is no man that hath left house, or brethren, or sisters, or father, or mother, or wife, or children, or lands, for My sake, and the gospel's, but He shall receive an hundredfold now in this time, houses, and brethren, and sisters, and mothers, and children, and lands, with persecutions; and in the world to come eternal life.
>
> —Mark 10:29–30 (KJV)

Last Steven Hall Family Picture, Mother's Day, 2013

CHAPTER 12

Hadassah

*W*ednesday, October 19, our daughter Bethany called at 9:00 p.m. to inform us that her OB appointment went well and that she's three centimeters dilated, seventy-five percent effaced, and that she's been having contractions for two weeks! The doctor didn't think she was going to make it much longer without delivering the baby.

Now, when we were told we were moving down here, and I accepted the job at US Renal Care, I had made a stipulation that I would have all of November and December off, specifically for the delivery and post cares of this baby since Bethany had three little boys and would need some help. We had already made plans to leave October 29, early morning, for just the entire month of November since I didn't have enough PTO to be out of work for two months. Well, with her phone call, I started calling my three bosses and asked if I could leave *now* even though I was on the next week's schedule. They all gave their blessing; all the while, Steve and I were packing for the trip. We left the next morning and got up to Bemidji, Minnesota on Friday afternoon. She didn't have Hadassah until the next Saturday morning, October 29 at 9:40. Go figure.

It was wonderful being there and being able to help do stuff that hadn't been done that they had tried to get done before the fall. Every time they would try to get stuff on their to-do list done, their basement would flood, for a total of flooding five times in one summer and early fall! She was *very* frustrated!

Anyway, we spent a wonderful six weeks at their home, getting lots of time with the grandsons and little Hadassah, as well as spending some time with our oldest daughter, Mary, and being there for her time of need as she went through several weeks of kidney stones. After the third trip to the ED, they decided to go in and stretch the ureter, to break up and extract the large stone stuck there and place a stent to assist the future stones that may occur. We were able to visit with Daniel and Hannah when they came over too.

One of the most amazing times while there was when Steve prayed over each of our three kids and their spouses and the three grandsons. He prayed over Hadassah after she arrived. When he prayed over each of them, they, no, *we* all cried! It was a sweet, sweet time with them, lifting them up to our and their heavenly Father!

When he prayed and poured oil on Franklin, Bethany's husband, the power of God just flooded that house! It was one of the most precious and intense times of spiritual warfare! After he prayed for Frank, he told Frank that he had to go to every door and window and anoint it with oil, and then they would both pray and thus secure and cover that house with the blood of Jesus! It was beyond powerful!

Of course, when we step out to do all that God has called us to do, the devil really doesn't like us! *At all!* He tried everything he could to stop and slow us down. I got some bronchial infection from Jeremiah and gave it to Steve, who gave it back to me; and so I was not at the top of my game for three to four of the six weeks we were there. It was pathetic, but we did stuff every day to help and watch the kids.

When Hadassah was home a couple of days, she started having colic-type issues. That poor little girl screamed bloody murder for hours both nights! Bethany and Frank were exhausted, and he had to go to work in the morning. I got up and took her for a while. I got into their rocker with her, and she shushed right up! We both slept in the chair for a couple of hours before I woke up and took her to her mommy to be nursed.

That next morning, we had a suspicion that she may be lactose intolerant like her brother Gabriel and several of her great aunts. Bethany cut out all dairy, and that night, no colic and no screaming! On days that Bethany forgot, those evenings were quite noisy, to say the least!

The times I had alone to spend with friends and prayer partners was limited but wonderful! God moved in mighty ways at every meeting, whether over coffee, tea, lunch, or just to have a quick chat, which always turned into a *long* chat. I even was able to help at the DaVita Dialysis units in Cass Lake and Park Rapids a few days.

I got most of their Thanksgiving meal cooked for their family gathering with Frank's family, but didn't stay. We had Thanksgiving dinner at the Bemidji Community Meal, which was held that year at Calvary Lutheran Church. The CMA chapter was always the group that did all the cooking as well as most of the serving and cleanup. We were able to visit our CMA chapter Common Bond buddies and many in the community that always show up to it, then went back to Bethany's for dessert and games with several of Frank's family. We had such a fun time! Many games and many laughs later, they all left, and we finished cleaning up the house from the event. For the first time in *many* years, we did *not* go to the Black Friday sales event at Walmart or anywhere else until Friday itself! It felt great!

In any case, we took Bethany and Hadassah with us and spent the last half of the morning and half of the afternoon and got all our Christmas shopping done. Good thing since we were having our family Christmas gathering the very next day. I'm glad I have taught our kids to be frugal. Bethany saves gift bags from all occasions and had a bunch available, so we didn't have to wrap anything at all!

Christmas for our family was November 26, 2016, and we had a fabulous time! Instead of my reading the Christmas story from the three Gospel books of the Bible, we went around the room with my starting the story and the next person continuing from where the last person left off. It was fun and got everyone involved. Even Scott, Mary's fiancé at the time. He and his two sons were there, our son Daniel and his wife Hannah, Frank and Bethany and their four kids, and of course Steve and I. We had a small turkey, which didn't leave any leftovers, and all the typical sides.

We left Monday morning, November 28, to start our journey home but with one added on stop. We headed to Kennett, Missouri, to visit Steve's Navy buddy Larry and his wife Linda. They'd had a very hard year that year, to say the least! She almost died of sepsis back in January 2016 and had since been in and out of the hospital like five times, including having a leg amputated in June. I was so glad we did. It was God ordained and so very needed by them. We were able to meet her mom that lived with them. We didn't get to stay long; we got there about 11:00 p.m. and had to leave around noon the next day, but we were really able to encourage them and lift them up! Larry seemed years younger when we left than when we had arrived!

We got back home to Kingwood, Texas, Tuesday night and got everything done, sorted, cleaned, etc. before I had to be back at work early Thursday morning. I worked Thursday through Saturday but got off just in time to go to our new CMA chapter's Christmas party near our apartment. That was wonderful!

Every week for the rest of the year, I worked six-day weeks again. It was difficult to get back in the swing of things after being gone and not working often for the last six weeks. I missed my family and those precious little grandkids so desperately! It was good to be home, but I missed those little hands and high-pitched voices saying, "I love you, Mamaw!" Breaks my heart just to think of it!

All this is to show how God knows what is going on at all times, and He has a plan. His timing is always perfect, and He knows what our hearts need and when they need it. He is such a good God! He supplies all our needs physically, spiritually, financially, emotionally, and mentally! All good and perfect gifts are from Him, our Father of lights!

> Every good gift and perfect gift is from above and
> cometh down from the Father of lights, with whom
> is no variableness, neither shadow of turning.
>
> —James 1:17

> Delight thyself also in the LORD; and He shall
> give thee the desires of thine heart.
>
> —Psalm 37:4

CHAPTER 13

The Kidney and I

*O*ctober 12. I had to get a recheck of my CTs that were done in the hospital back in April. I got it done, and before I left the facility (GO Imaging on the FM 1960), I had a copy in my hand, which included the CTs from April! Cool. That cancelled my having to deal with getting the copy *at* the hospital. The next week, I was able to drop it off at Dr. Ira Krause's office.

Anyway, I was finally able to get to my follow-up appointment with Dr. Krause on Tuesday, December 20. Steve and I scooted our chairs near the computer screen as the doctor loaded the CD of my CT scans from October and April. What we saw changed the remainder of the year—well, and my life. The big dark area in the left kidney was not the angiomyolipoma (a usually large cyst that can hemorrhage but is basically harmless) that he was expecting and really hoping for. Instead, it was probably renal cell carcinoma, and it was a large tumor.

He said he would show the scan to some colleagues for second and third opinions; but if it was, he would want to remove the kidney completely as the tumor was just about throughout the entire kidney, starting at the center. He had us make an appointment for the next Thursday, just before New Year's weekend. I had asked if we did in fact have to do a radical nephrectomy, would it be possible to do the surgery the next week due to my insurance ending at the end of the year. He said there was no way that would be possible as it is just next week, and due to insurances, there are a lot of hoops to jump through, and scheduling at this late in the month was impossible due to many elective surgeries that have been scheduled for months already. Probably, we should expect the first or second week of January.

Well, with my insurance ending, my new job, which I start Christmas Eve, won't have me covered until the first of February. He said we should be able to wait till February as I've had this tumor since April. We left the office feeling optimistic and believing God for a miracle, and that they would not find any cancer—period!

I worked every day after that appointment, and most days were long hours. Friday was my last full-time day for US Renal Care. And of course, it was the last Friday before Christmas, so traffic was dreadful, and I got home a bit late. I had to work Saturday at my new full-time job at Dialyspa, which is doing the acute dialysis at the Kingwood Medical Center near our apartment, so I went to bed early.

I noticed as I was turning off my phone that I had two new voice mail messages from some weird unfamiliar phone numbers, so I went ahead and turned off my phone to charge while I slept. Saturday, Christmas Eve, we worked like crazy! The doctors there seemed to want every single person that came in the ED to have a dialysis treatment! Yes, that's an exaggeration, but we ended up with over twenty-two patients on our "slow day" schedule of staff! So after working a very long, grueling day, I was not doing *anything* else but enjoying seeing the Christmas lights in our new little community, Kings Manor, and a few other subdivisions in Kingwood with my husband. We had a great evening and saw some amazing light exhibits that were astounding, went home, ate pizza, and went to bed.

We got up Christmas morning, had our Christmas event, opened our gifts to each other and those that were sent to us through the mail or by others, had breakfast, and got ready for church. On the way to church while Steve drove, I got out my phone and listened to my new messages. Both were from the doctor and were from his personal cell phone and home phone. He wanted me to call him immediately when I got those messages. It was imperative he speak with me as soon as possible, no matter the time. Well, that's not ever a good message to hear from a doctor, no matter when you get that message!

However, it was Christmas morning, and I was not going to ruin his family's Christmas. So as he gave his cell number, I texted him who I was and that I had just gotten his messages, but I would not ruin his family's Christmas by calling, so I asked him to call me that afternoon or evening when his Christmas stuff was done and over. Ours was done, and once church was over, our Christmas was complete; and dinner was with our two best friends Roger and Ara, so a phone call from him would be fine.

Church was great, and dinner was fabulous: again, a turkey with all the trimmings, and they brought chocolate lava cake that they baked in our oven while we ate. They left shortly after for a short family thing with Roger's son, but they would be back to have dessert and coffee and play some games. Steve teased about enjoying a long nap while they were gone. They left at 5:00 p.m., Steve conked out at 5:10 p.m., and I called Bethany and the kids to see how their Christmas went.

I hung up the phone at 5:25; and at 5:27, the doctor called. He said the three doctors he showed my scans to all agree that it is in fact renal cell carcinoma; and after comparing the CDs, it seems to be quite aggressive, so he wants to do a radical left nephrectomy that coming Friday, December 30, due to the speed in which that tumor had been growing. Wow!

The next couple of hours were a whirlwind of phone calls and texts. I had to inform all of our kids and my family and then my godparents and friends. I hated calling on Christmas evening, but I was working the rest of the week, and I didn't want them to get a phone call Friday, saying, "Sorry, Melody died in surgery today!" and their responses like, "Surgery? *What surgery?* Why weren't we/wasn't I told?" So I called and spoke to each for a bit, made sure they were sitting down or not driving, then told that the doctor called a little bit ago.

The next bunches of calls were to my three bosses. During that time, Ara and Roger had called, but I couldn't answer, so she texted, thinking we were actually still napping, saying that they'll come over some other time for dessert. When I had a chance to check my texts, I saw it and replied, "We'd *really* like it if you could come tonight anyway, even for a few minutes. The doctor called tonight."

Well, that was all it took. She looked at Roger as they were pulling into their driveway and said, "Just shut the coops up [they raise organic chickens]. We've got to get back to Steve and Melody's. The doctor called her tonight!" They got there and were told the outcome of "the call."

While we had dessert, we made plans for a few fundraisers. We prayed together and sent them home at 11:00 p.m. as we *all* had to work the next morning, except Steve, but he was helping with another ministry that Monday.

The next week was a blur of activity. I worked Monday and Tuesday and got off early due to not having many patients. I was able to run to the Memorial Hermann Northeast Hospital in Humble for preadmission and presurgery checkups. I was then told that in order to have the surgery on Friday morning, I had to pay $1,460.63 of the estimated $5,695 (which was my portion after my insurance paid the rest) by end of day on Thursday, or they'd cancel the surgery. We didn't have that kind of money, especially since I hardly worked in November and had a lot of bills, and Steve still didn't have a job! I posted the need on Facebook and put the fact that if I didn't come up with this amount by Thursday, I wouldn't be having my surgery. I was blessed so mightily over the next little more than a day; by early morning Thursday, I had the entire down payment amount in my newly created PayPal account! Praise God!

I was on call on Wednesday, so I had the daytime off and got to go out to lunch with Daniel and Hannah when they got into town, then go home and play games till I got called in Wednesday evening and was there through the night till about 7:00 Thursday morning. While I was at work, our longtime family friends got in at about 11:00 p.m.

When I got off work, I went home, made an amazing dinner in the Crock-Pot for that evening, and we all got ready, went to the hospital to pay that down payment, then headed to Galveston to my favorite beach since we've been down here, Jamaica Beach.

When we left there, Steve and I had to stop at the Hobby Airport to pick up my mom, Beverly, and one of my sisters Antoinette. On our way to the airport, the doctor's office called and told me I had to be on clear liquids from that point till midnight and then NPO. I was so bummed! I had fixed this *amazing* pork loin dinner that had been cooking *all day long*. When we got home, I made the gravy, veggies, and all the other things; served dinner to everybody; then sat down with them, drinking my chicken broth. Sad!

Surgery day. Before we left the apartment, I made sure to kiss every single person in my home goodbye and tell them I loved them and admonished them to continue following Jesus with all their heart, mind, body, and soul! I also wished our son, "Happy twenty-fourth birthday, honey!" as it was his twenty-fourth birthday (one he will *never* forget).

When we got to the hospital, the front desk people weren't there, as we had been told. I called the number the little note said to call and got my party and several others that came in after us in, but I had to make sure all were out of the enclosed waiting room. When I came out of said waiting room, it was a ghost town! No one was anywhere I looked! So I had to call the number again! Just as another nurse came to get me and the next couple of people that came in, the front desk volunteer came in.

I was the first case of the day, and Pastor Mike showed up to pray with us. He came over especially to see us from his ranch in West Texas. Well, he had to do a business something but said he couldn't leave until he came to see and pray with us! How awesome was that? It is such a privilege to have such an amazing pastor! Our church is a testimony to how he lives his life close to God and striving to follow God in *all* his ways and with a heart after God and, therefore, *missions!* He is a great man I am proud to call friend!

When the doctor came in to meet the family and mark on my body where he was going in to do the surgery, Pastor Mike left. When Dr. Krause asked if there was anything else he could do, I told him that I wanted a picture of the kidney once it was out. Had I really thought about it, I'd have asked for a video! He looked at me like I was crazy! He chuckled and said I wasn't serious, but I convinced him that I was very serious. I wanted to see the inside of it as well. So he said he would get the pathologist to come in and dissect it so he can lay it flat and get me a picture of the kidney laid open. It was a great picture, let me tell you!

Just before 7:00 a.m., the circulating nurse Bernadette came in with a technician and said they were going to give me some versed and something else and then take me to the OR. I kissed Steve, my mom, and sister, and then I don't remember anything else until I was in my room that afternoon.

That day, the doctor said I was to get up and walk as soon as I could—by the next morning, at the latest. I remember seeing Steve, Mom, Annie, Daniel, and Hannah in my room, and I remember pain at my abdomen. Over the next day and a half, I had several visitors from our Christian Motorcyclists Association chapter, Disciples of Christ out of Porter, Texas, number 1339, as well as a few from our church, Crossroads Fellowship, Houston, Texas. I was blessed and was able to bless the staff that took care of me while I was a patient. A few were Christians, and we had a wonderful time blessing each other and lifting up the name of our heavenly Father!

They were all amazed at how fast I was recovering and my body was healing. The doctor said I was recovering at a miraculous rate! God is so good! He discharged me on Sunday afternoon, January 1, 2017. I hardly needed anything for pain. The first twelve hours, I had only used my Dilaudid pump only five times. When they came to disconnect it, they encouraged me to take one last dose as I was starting to do my walking. The rest of the time, if I needed anything for pain, I had Tylenol or ibuprofen. That's it for pain killers after my surgery. Again, God is good!

I started walking laps around the unit I was on; and by that evening, I was walking at an average pace even though I just had major surgery. They couldn't believe it! They thought I was cutting through areas, but when one of the nurses followed me on my "walk about," as I called it, she commented how I was "trucking along like a mall walker," not even cutting the corners. I think I ended up doing over thirty laps and doing stuff in my room without pain or any other problem or issue before being released to go home on Sunday afternoon.

Steve got a call on Friday, December 30, 2016, and was interviewed by Kroger Grocery Store and asked if he would come in that following Tuesday for a face-to-face interview, which he did and got hired on the spot. He started Thursday, January 5, 2017, in the meat department, and he has loved his job.

So for the next three weeks, I was off and stayed home or went to the Livestrong Group at the YMCA nearest us that our friend Ara is in charge of. That is a wonderful opportunity to have a cancer support group, get three months of free YMCA membership, build relationships and encourage each other, and build our strength and stamina since all the members are cancer survivors and a support person (usually spouse or family member) in some phase of post diagnosis. It was a wonderful experience, and God provided a lot of chances to minister every single day.

My mom and sister were able to keep an eye on me while Steve worked; and as I got stronger, I was able to take them to a few places around the area and enjoy our time together, not to mention all the movies we were able to watch together! We had a *The Hobbit* and *The Lord of the Rings* (extended edition) marathon that took three days. It was fabulous!

The first Wednesday of the year, we all went to church and had a wonderful service. After service, on our way out, I was hit by this wave of pain I hadn't experienced until then. *Wow!* It took my breath away, and I grabbed hold of the rail surrounding the walkway for dear life, thinking I was about to collapse. Steve came out then and pulled the car up as close as he could, then came over and helped me to it and to get in. It was so good, though, to be in the house of the Lord! I unfortunately worried a few people, but Pastor was sure glad to see me.

Sunday, the eighth of January, I had a spaghetti feed fundraiser that was to help with some of the costs having this cancer had incurred. Steve and I went to Kroger's and bought the meat and such to make the spaghetti and garlic bread, about twenty dollars. I had several people prepay, which was what we had asked for, but few came for the food. We had about eight come total, and those came two at a time, or one would come to pick up two to go. That day, I was on my feet a lot of the day, and I made everything. I felt it the next day. Oofdah! My abdomen was sore and tight, and I was exhausted. It was a good stretch out of my typical day up to that point. We made about two hundred dollars.

I have no idea why I had to go through all of this and no idea what He has in store, but His word in Romans 8:28 promises that He will work all things together for the good for those who are in Christ Jesus. Sometimes, it feels like it was a passing dream in the night, but then I see the five-inch scar on my left side, and I am hit with the reality of what had truly transpired and what could have happened. He has plans for me that I haven't done yet, like writing this book. It was such a quick experience with cancer!

Tuesday before Christmas 2016, I got told that what was seen on my CT scans may be cancer. Sunday, Christmas day 2016, at 5:27 p.m., CST, I am informed that what was seen on my scans was in fact cancer, a very aggressive renal cell carcinoma to be exact. Friday, December 26, 2016, I had an emergency radical left nephrectomy, which is the removal of a kidney, in the early morning; and by noon, I was cancer free! Praise the Lord! I am healed at "a miraculous rate," according to my medical team and Dr. Ira Krause, and I was released to our home on Sunday, January 1, 2017 in the early afternoon. Dr. Krause said he had never seen anything like it in all the years of his practice. To hardly have any pain at all, and I was up for short periods that night, and then making laps around the hospital floor the morning after surgery—he couldn't believe what a quick recovery I was making!

It was wonderful to be able to spend time with family and relax. For the almost two years prior to this, I had been working between six and seven days per week on average. Our finances were okay, but there is such a desperate need for nurses, especially RNs, in the dialysis world. Since coming back to work, after a mere three weeks off for medical leave, I have only worked one six-day week and no seven-day weeks.

One thing I learned through this is that a job and career are wonderful, especially if you love your work, but no one is going to look out for you and keep you healthy other than yourself and your spouse. If you get sick, you won't be able to work at all for who knows how long and maybe end up never being able to return to work. Keep yourself healthy, and you can work at the top of your game for many years to come. Keeping yourself healthy isn't just about working sensible hours but also getting good rest and spending down time having fun with family and friends and taking time to relax on your own like taking a long bubble bath; reading a good book; going for a long walk *and* smelling the flowers; taking a nice ride in your car, on a bicycle, or on a motorcycle; and enjoying the beauty that God made for us to enjoy regularly.

As much as your work is your place of ministry, your family is your first and foremost ministry of all. Your family is your responsibility to teach—by both actions and words—of the love of God. We can't minister, work, or teach without being there. We will stand before Him one day and give an account as to why we didn't or get to hear those words we long to hear: "Well done, you good and faithful servant!" I do know that He will be using this experience as He does all our experiences sooner or later for His glory and to draw others back to Himself!

> But He was wounded for our transgressions, He was
> bruised for our iniquities: the chastisement of our peace
> was upon Him; and with His stripes we are healed.
> —Isaiah 53:5 (KJV)

> For I will restore health unto thee, and I will
> heal thee of thy wounds, saith the LORD.
> —Jeremiah 30:17a (KJV)

This is my kidney "butterflied" after surgery.
The yellow corn-looking things are nephrons.
The white and black areas are the cancer.

CHAPTER 14

Hurricane Harvey

August 2018

*H*urricane Harvey has been deemed the biggest catastrophe that has ever hit the Houston area to date and largest natural disaster in America. It destroyed more than Hurricane Katrina did by far. There will be areas that were devastated that will never be even close to what it was prior to this disaster. I want to tell you our story of being hit by Hurricane Harvey. We were one family of hundreds of thousands. Each family had a similar yet very different experience with it. We were so blessed that no one in our family lost their life or even limbs! Thank You, Jesus!

While we were living in the middle of it, I decided to keep the texts and Facebook entries for remembering the details for a possible future book, so the texts and Facebook things I mention will be in *blue* as they are the actual word-for-word renditions.

We had just moved in to our beautiful new townhome at the Town Center Apartments of Kingwood up near the intersection of West Lake Houston and Kingwood Drive. Our townhome was directly behind the Kingwood Public Library, and our back patio faced a beautiful, peaceful bubbling brook. Our son Daniel and his wife, Hannah, had moved into the complex into a regular apartment on the ground floor a few buildings away from ours about two months before us.

We had been enjoying spending time with them and helping Hannah with the heat and keeping her active as she had just found out she was pregnant in mid/late May. We went swimming almost literally every single day, unless it was closed for cleaning or pouring down rain.

We had an attached garage and a humongous gourmet kitchen, which was my pride and joy of our new home. The living/dining area was completely open to the open kitchen, so it was really one gigantic room with all brand-new stainless steel appliances and a nine-foot long, four-foot wide island with the sink in the middle of it. I had so many cupboards and cabinets and even a small pantry that I was hard placed to fill them all. I could, at the touch of a button, turn on and dim or brighten lights under the cabinets or above the island, which was track lighting with adjustable light fixtures to aim wherever you would like them to brighten. We had a wonderful side by side refrigerator with a water and ice dispenser in the front of the freezer door, which was Steve's pride and joy!

We had been in for just about three weeks when the news started talking about this tropical storm they were calling Harvey. We still had more than half of our stuff in boxes and totes in the garage. We weren't rushing to move any of it in as it was a smaller place than we've been in for almost thirty years. We wanted to arrange things just right; and with both of us working, we had limited time to do so.

We just finished grocery shopping and stocking up our new refrigerator with freezer and our stand-up freezer in the garage with a bunch of beef; chicken; fish; seafood; turkey; bacon; frozen vegetables; frozen fruits; and frozen entrees like ravioli, lasagnas, etc.—oh, and Steve's favorite: ice cream! Our cupboards and pantry were finally stocked with the dry goods and all the beans and rice I wanted for the next couple of months.

We were planning on being life group leaders for our church small groups, so I was planning the big meals for when we had several couples/families at our place. We were set, or so we thought. Not being from this area, we asked people that have lived in the area for a while to find out how they have fared with things like tropical storms turned hurricanes in the past. All of them had said that they have never flooded but have had power outages for up to three and a half weeks. Well, we may lose some of our food, but we have neighbors that can store some if it gets bad, and we can cook up a bunch of it on the grill that Steve went out and bought on Friday, or so that's what we planned for the situation.

On Thursday afternoon, Dialyspa asked for two of the Kingwood Hospital Acutes Team to volunteer to be on lockdown starting Friday and to expect to be in lockdown for up to a full week. Lockdown is literally what it sounds like. The hospital locked all doors, and there was one entrance left open at the emergency room for patients and staff to *come in* only. Once in, as it was unsafe outside, you couldn't leave, not even to stand in the parking lot. It sounds mean, but it truly was for everyone's safety.

I volunteered with Steve's approval since I do not have little ones at home, and I know my family is ready as well as can be expected, and they all are strong, capable people to get through whatever life throws at them. There are so many young nurses that have little ones at home and have never been through any kind of severe/catastrophic weather that if they were at work, they would be so sidetracked with worry for their kids and/or spouse and families that they would not have been much good to keep patients safe and continue their various healing processes.

Of course, months later, Steve told me that he had agreed to it because he knew I would be in a much safer place, and that he wouldn't have to worry about me, bless his little pea-pickin' heart! Sneaky man! I was told by my supervisor to go shopping and get enough food to last me up to the full week and try to get things that don't need to be refrigerated or cooked as power may not be available. I stocked up on trail mixes, nuts, dried and fresh fruits, meats that are cured and don't need refrigeration, some crackers, and a few microwave meals that I could use while we had power over the next day or two. The nice thing was they said they would reimburse me for it since I am working. What a blessing!

They also paid us around the clock, twenty-four hours each day we were there. Granted, it was just the two of us for a while, so we were actually working very long hours and only off to sleep for a few hours for several days until more nurses were able to come in as days went by and the weather started clearing up and water started receding. My company Dialyspa started doing the lockdown a day before the HCA Kingwood Medical Center did as we were also able and needed to give dialysis treatments to any patients whose home clinic was unable to do their treatment.

The following is from my Facebook post on Friday, August 25, 2017:

> 1046 "They say this COULD be the worst Hurricane that has hit Texas in 47 years. Pray for Texas, Houston, and no flooding! We probably won't be able to contact anyone for a few days, but we will try to text, call or if nothing else post some kind of updates daily. If you see update please forward them to family... Love ya'll and will be in hospital lock-in til Sunday morning at least... Steve, Daniel, and Hannah will be at the apts...both are bottom floor...ugh"

That morning, Friday, August 25, I was called to start doing dialysis treatments before 5:00 a.m. while I was still at home getting my stuff together. Upon my arrival, I was shown where we were to sleep, and since it was only me, another dialysis nurse, and a patient care technician, we had our choice of cots. I found out later that she went home, so it was only me. HCA bought one hundred or so military cots and set them up in the community room over by the HR office. I picked my cot and then moved it to be against a wall near an electric outlet so I could plug in my CPAP machine so that I could sleep and not stop breathing.

That day was very busy! We had almost all of our regularly scheduled staff there as Harvey was just hitting landfall over by Corpus Christi in Port Aransas and Port O'Connor, so nothing had hit our area yet. It hit those areas with winds at about 130 miles per hour. I will say, I don't remember a time since 9/11 where just about every single person was watching television. I mean, every room that had a person in it had the television on some news coverage of Harvey and its progress.

That first night of our lockdown was pretty uneventful. I worked overnight a little bit, but on Saturday, August 26, things started hopping at the hospital. That was the day that the hurricane hit the Houston area, and it stayed there for about four full days! Some news stations said that over one half of all of Houston was under a minimum of one half to two feet of nasty floodwater. There was so much water that it caused Houston to actually sink during the storm; but thankfully, it rebounded after the waters receded. We started taking in a lot of patients that day. I found out that we did twenty-one in that twenty-four-hour period alone. I worked very late that day.

We were told that as we were in lockdown, the meals were being provided at the cafeteria for all staff, including the contracted staff like me. That was a nice blessing! They prepared a nice variety for every meal and included a bowl of oatmeal with toppings and OJ or whatever to drink for breakfast, side salad and/or soup, as well as a drink for the other meals. Oh yes, and there was always a dessert for lunch and dinner! We could give our badge to a coworker to pick up our meals if we were not able to go ourselves, which was wonderful, knowing how full our schedules were with the extra patients. I didn't have to eat the dried goods I had brought for a little while longer anyway.

During the week, I was able to get to know many of the kitchen workers, including Tim, a four-star chef that was in charge of it. He had ordered extra just in case a lockdown would happen and thought about the length of time before he would be able to get more shipments in during and after the hurricane. Smart guy! He had plenty left when the trucks were able to start rolling in again around September 1. He, as well as all the administration and department heads, pitched in to serve us. They also did some kind of activity or special treat every couple of nights. The kitchen, with all their help, did a great job!

The following is the post from Facebook from Saturday, August 26, 2017:

> 1251 "Starting day 2 the hospital is officially on "Lock-Down" and have called in almost all staff to come join in the fun so they have enough staff to cover every shift and keep the staff rotating for rest periods. They have about 100 military cots and have designated several pt rooms for us to shower in.
>
> When I talk about "all at home" that means Steve, Daniel and Hannah going forward. Soooo, all at home are well and apts are safe at this moment yet our beautiful, bubbling brook out our back patio is quickly becoming a roaring river. Our apt is on "red alert" to say the least. Will keep ya'll updated as I can. So far, so good. Pray for slower rain and

that Harvey will dissipate quickly. Tornadoes are
all over the place as well, but not near Kingwood.
Love you guys!"

I worked a regular schedule on Saturday as we only ended up doing thirteen treatments. After work, I took the games I brought and found a break room that some staff were hanging out in, and we played games. They had no idea what Pass the Pigs was about! I went to my cot that night about midnight. That was the last night we had power.

Sometime during the night, we lost power and went to backup generators, which meant that only the things that were imperative were running, and things that were plugged in that were necessary had to be plugged into the "red" electrical sockets. That also meant that I now had no CPAP machine available. Those poor people in the community room sleeping with me; I can imagine how loud I was. Anytime someone had to charge their phone, they had to do it while in a room with a patient or at the nurse's station with computers running.

Our cell phones were handy little gadgets, let me tell you! We used them for our flashlights, alarm clocks, games, trying to keep up with what's going on outside in the storm, and communication with our job as well as family and friends, except any communication was hit-and-miss for the week. The best bet was texting. Phone lines and cell towers were down all over the greater Houston area, and the ones that were up and running were bombarded with calls going out as well as coming in. Most days during this week, if you were able to get a phone call and texts, that was a great day!

Sunday, August 27, was a busier-than-usual day for a Sunday but less busy than I had anticipated it to be. We did only seven patients. Now that means that the two of us were quite busy. Our dialysis unit at the hospital can only hold four patients and only two nurses at a time. Since there was only the two of us, one of us—myself—had to go do the treatments that had to be done bedside, like in ICU or ICC. We were quite busy that day for just us.

The following is the Facebook post from Sunday, August 27, 2017:

> 1259 (12:59pm) "Day 3. We are well and apts are still safe and dry. I'm in Lock-Down at the hospital still and expected not to be able to leave til Tuesday at the earliest. Glad I packed for 5 days... I'm working and the morale of both pts and staff seems good at the time. Pts BP is up due to watching the news and seeing footage of their home areas. It's a mess out there. The cot is getting to be more comfortable as the nights go by, LOL. Still better than the floor. Love you guys! We'll keep you posted as much as possible. We are now under a Tornado Warning and have had to prepare all pts rooms accordingly for safety. So not a fun day! God is still good and He IS still in control!"

And another post:

> 1452 (2:52pm) "God has a great sense of humor. I woke up last night several times with a different song in my head each time. "Loves like a hurricane, I am a tree..." "let the river flow"... "I've got Peace like a river"...and the last one, "so let the storms rage high, let dark clouds rise, they don't worry me, for I'm sheltered safe within the arms of God"... I looked up and said, "Really? You would put THOSE songs in my head! I could hear Him chuckle... Sorry, that was thunder! Lol. God is so good! Fear not everybody, God's got this!" Our God is a good God and throughout the entire ordeal, He was constantly showing Himself faithful and present for He promised in His word to NEVER leave us or forsake us!!

Another post from 5:17 p.m.:

> (1717) "I just heard from Steve. All on our side of
> the apts are on standby for evacuation d/t flooding."

At this point, my family was okay. They had power and cable and all the regular things for their daily life. They went to work but were having very low business. Most grocery stores were empty of food, bread, all milks, and all waters. When I went shopping for my trail mixes on Thursday, most stores were already empty. There were few deliveries made in the last three days; and when they did get a delivery, they were sold out within the hour.

Word traveled fast, and people were stocking up for the antici-pated three-to-four-week period of need. Daniel had gone to work for a few hours on Saturday, as scheduled, but there were only like five or six employees total that showed up. They opened anyway and actually had a few customers, although it was drive-through only. After a few hours of hardly any business, the two management ladies sent everyone home except Daniel, who had to clean the grill to keep any fires from happen-ing. That particular Whataburger had just opened about four weeks prior to Hurricane Harvey's hitting. Everything was top-of-the-line, and the grill was extra large, just as he had requested. Daniel was the first and the last person to cook anything in that store. That was the last time Daniel saw that place without its being in many feet of water. The kids, Daniel, and Hannah played games and watched movies with Steve over the week-end when power was on, but it was intermittent over the weekend.

As of Monday, things changed drastically. The following is a post from Monday, August 28, 2017:

> 0605am: "Day 4. Dialysis unit been running all night in preparation for the onslaught of dialysis pts that have no clinic to do their treatment at. I expect the unit to be running nonstop for this next few days. Haven't heard from Steve and his phone was off last time I tried. I live (this was edited to say "love" then put back to "live". I figured God

had a reason for the autocorrect!) the songs God keeps putting in my heart. Today's is," and when my heart is overwhelmed; lead me to the rock that is higher than I." God IS good! God loves YOU!

The following is a post from my wonderful pastor Mike Allard of Crossroads Fellowship:

0717 Mike Allard August 28, 2017 · Atascocita, TX
June 2001 was the first week I started pastoring this church. With only a few days into pastoring we had tropical storm Allison. 35 homes in our church were either flooded or destroyed. It was devastating and heart breaking. Many of you remember the horrible experience that was. At that time, we were told it was a 500 year flood. If that was a 500 year flood then this is a 1000 year flood. It was the most trying time of my life. However, it was not the end. This is not the end. God had a greater story to write then and God has a greater story to write now.
There were some powerful lessons that disaster taught us. We learned that we can survive the worst. We realized in the middle of crisis we are stronger together. We prayed to God. We gave and encouraged each other to press on. We can do it again. The Lord is with us even when we can't see Him. When other communities in America are fighting and torn apart by politics this is time for Houston to stand tall and stand together. Let's join together and reach out to each other. So look for those opportunities to give to those around you. What a great day it is to serve the Lord and to serve each other.

Daniel was scheduled to work his second job on Monday at the Exxon owned by Timewise located diagonally from that Whataburger at West Lake Houston and Kingwood Drive; but as power was out in more places than it was on, he called to see if they were open. They had no power and still wanted him to come in to run the store, although they had no way of ringing up any sales, no gas pumps worked, no coolers or air-conditioning worked, and they had no camera coverage for safety as people were already starting to loot places. He told them he wasn't coming in as there was absolutely nothing he could do to work; and after discussing it with the manager, the manager agreed and just locked the place up. That was the last time anyone was in that store/ gas station until about a month later. It was actually one of the first places of business in that area to open after Harvey dissipated. Due to the amount of rain that had fallen already at this point, the streets were flooding, but not like the flooding we were about to witness!

I was notified by one of the HCA nurses that the housekeeping department, EVS, was offering laundry services to the staff in lockdown. We had to bring our stuff in a single bag with our name and department on it and go pick it up the next day. They would do a single load per staff member; no white load and load of colors, just a single load for whatever was in the bag. I was thrilled! I had just started planning washing my used clothes by hand in a bathroom but had no way of drying them.

We did twenty-one dialysis treatments that day and had a very small crew of nurses to do them. We got them done, but this is when we started sleeping for a few hours and then doing a couple of shifts of patients before we slept for a few hours again. This is when things got fun, so to speak, in our community. During the early part of the day, Daniel and Hannah were over at our place, keeping a watchful eye on my little bubbling brook as it turned into an angry roaring river about two miles wide with superfast currents. Hannah occasionally would text me pictures of it throughout the day.

The following is a post from Hannah, my daughter-in-law. At 5:19 p.m., she posted,

> We cant leave even if we wanted to roads are flooded and cops are stopping everyone. Power is out everywhere so Daniel is home with me. His dad is bugging out at our place. Its his apartment that has the brook now river behind his place.

Steve ended up evacuating our place to Daniel and Hannah's an hour or so after the above picture was taken as water was at our patio doors. He put as much of our stuff as he could on top of counters, cabinets, tables, the bed, shelves in the closets and garage and packed a suitcase for the two of us before he left. He took the suitcase and his CPAP machine with him as well as our My Pillows. That was the last time he saw our place before Hurricane Harvey wiped us out.

Power was out until Saturday sometime while we were sorting through the stuff, if I recall. So he went over, and they played games until it was too dark to see, then they went to bed. Steve slept on the couch. That night, a little after midnight, Hannah woke up screaming about someone hitting her car out in the parking lot, which woke Steve up. He got off the couch into water! He looked out the window; and though there was a car that had barely missed her car, her tires were under water. He got everyone up, and they packed up what they could, put it in their SUVs, and tried to leave the apartment complex.

When they came around the corner from their regular parking spots, their headlights illuminated a huge several-foot wall of water coming at them. They threw the vehicles in reverse, aimed them to the landscaping, and gunned it so they drove up into the lawn into the bushes so they were on a high pointed slope. They jumped out with their suitcases and started running up the stairs to see if someone would let them in.

It was now close to 1:30 a.m. I was still performing treatments on patients at this time, so I only received clipped texts from Daniel keeping me somewhat abreast of all that was going on. I didn't know until afternoon, but they found someone, an off duty police officer and his wife with a new baby, to let them stay the rest of the night. He radioed into the dispatcher to have boats start heading their way so they can evacuate after it was light. I prayed for daylight for my family. I texted my giant group text to pray for them and gave a rundown of what was happening at our homes. That's the last I heard from anyone until about noon Tuesday, August 29.

Throughout the night, flooding was hitting homes from two different directions. One was the flooding coming in from the nearby lakes, rivers, bayous, and creeks, while the other was a bit more unusual. No one really thinks about what happens to drains and plumbing during extreme flooding, at least most people I've ever talked to have. The second way the flooding hit was from within their homes. Flooding was coming up through the drains in the sinks and tubs, up the toilets, and into washing machines as well as dishwashers.

We have some very good friends from our church, Sam and Katie. They are a beautiful and wonderful family with three adorable kids. Sam is a police officer in Kingwood, Texas; and of course, he was on duty during this time of disaster for our community. That young man kept calling or texting me to check on me and my family. Monday night, when it was getting bad and I had received the text from Daniel about the wall of water and not being able to leave the complex, he texted to check up on us again, so I told him about the situation. He was with some of the national guard and was in a military Hummer with a snorkel. He told them, and they were going to go rescue them.

They got out into the water from near where Sharky's Restaurant was, and the force of the water slammed into that vehicle and started washing it away. It took them a little while to regain control and get out of the current. They tried a few more times but to no avail. He was so frustrated! He even called for others to try to get them from the other side, but they couldn't either. He texted me back and told me of the problem and all that had been attempted on their behalf. He was so sorry, but my family would have to wait until daylight the next morning before any possible opportunity of rescue could happen, but he would keep me posted.

When my family woke up and were notified that boats were coming, they all grabbed their suitcases and had to find a safe place that the boats could get to so they could load people in. That officer and my guys started the trail, and everyone in the complex followed them. Daniel was barefoot, and poor Hannah was swimming since the water was over five feet deep. That water was revolting. It was mainly brown and had sewage, lead, arsenic—every toxin in the area—and was extremely thick and gritty. It also had a horrible odor.

Steve noticed several snakes swimming along with the people. He hates snakes with a passion, so he kept his focus on keeping Hannah above water and following the lead of the officer and Daniel while praying for protection the whole time. He kept the fact about swimming with the water moccasins to himself until much later. That was a very good decision too as Hannah more than likely would've freaked out!

They finally found a place and had a great system down swiftly for boats docking, loading, leaving, repeating, and keeping everyone and everything moving smooth and fast. Several boatloads later, the three were the last so they went door-to-door on the second and third floors to ensure no one was left behind, period. A little elderly woman was so scared and kept telling Daniel that she couldn't get into "that thing," so he told her, "Sure you can! It's this easy," at which point he picked her up and set her in the boat. Problem solved!

He refused to allow anyone to stay behind with no power, no communication, and quite very possibly no available help for several days, especially the elderly and ladies with kids. Hannah was in the first boat available for adults; and because she was pregnant, the doctor upon her arrival at the other end of the evacuation site sent her by a volunteer to my hospital Kingwood Medical Center!

After the entire complex was completely evacuated, they got into the last boat. Thank you to the Cajun Navy for rescuing my family by the way; and when they reached the evacuation site, they were told to *run* to the vehicles ahead as the water was continuing to rise, and the area they were using by the community center and post office were about to flood as well. They were told they were being Life Flighted to Dallas. Daniel said no; he was going wherever they had sent his wife. They found out it was KMC, so they sent him in the front seat of an ambulance to meet her there.

So then, they tried to send Steve to Dallas, and he refused as well. He told them I worked at KMC, and he was going to my hospital where there was a vehicle that he would use to take all of them to a safe place out of town. They grudgingly agreed as long as he was sure and sent him to KMC in a regular truck full of doctors and nurses that were heading to that hospital to help with all the influx of patients the hurricane was causing.

While this was going on, Tuesday was extremely busy. It was the busiest day during the disaster with twenty-six patients. I was finishing a treatment and was able to go take a few hours of a break, so a nap was finally going to happen! As I slept in the dark community room, my coworker Rowena came and woke me up. She was trying to do it quietly and not to alarm me, but once she whispered, "Your husband is in the ER," I bolted up and said, "What?" in a loud voice. She quietly repeated herself and, looking around and seeing how very dark it was, I stripped down right there from my pajama shorts and top and threw my sundress on as I went out the door telling her,

"Thank you," as I went. Poor Rowena saw way more of me than she ever bargained for—she and anyone else awake and looking. I don't even want to know! I didn't even think about that. I just needed to get to Steve and see if he was okay since he was in the ER.

I walked as fast as I could; and with my long legs, I was practically running through the back area of the hospital, taking the back section to the ER. I came through the ER doors into the waiting room as professionally as I could under the circumstances. I finally saw him by a window and ran into his arms! It was so good to feel his arms around me! Like the Lord, who knows what we are going through to the absolute depths and has promised to never leave us or forsake us, we know we can always run into His arms that are always ready to hold His beloved child! He also knows what we have need of even before we do, so He sent my awesome husband to me just at the right time to hold me! God is so very good! I hadn't seen him since early Friday morning and hadn't heard from him since Monday when he evacuated our home to go to our son's apartment. He was here, and he was safe! Praise the Lord for His mercy!

So after we stopped hugging, I started looking around for Daniel and Hannah but didn't see them. Steve noticed and told me that they were on the labor and delivery side of the hospital as she needed to be checked out since she scraped her belly flipping into the evacuation boat and was sore. The doctor that sent her to KMC wanted her checked out just to be sure everything was good. The lucky ducks were in a big exam room with a huge shower and were both using it to get the muck that stuck to them as they waded and swam through the filthy flood waters. Once they emerged, we all hugged; and finding out that they hadn't eaten anything since last night, I had them come with me to the KMC cafeteria and put their appetites into the very capable hands of Tim, the four-star chef.

At 8:48 p.m., I posted on Facebook,

> Day 5—All are here at the hospital with me. Safe
> and sound but drenched. Had a boat ride. Steve
> and Daniel helped load about 200 people to the
> boats before they were told it's their turn. Thank

you Jesus! They're safe! Everything else is gone but a suitcase per couple.

Have a couple of hours of "rest" or "downtime" before I hit the floor with pts again. Sitting in the Chapel that has NO cross, btw, I was singing and praising the Lord for His mercy and grace and getting my family somewhere safe (They are at our CMA chapter president's house) and then just praying for His strength and to be Jesus to all I come across during this time of crisis (I'm very tired and don't want to be crabby or short with people and miss any opportunities and Divine Appointments), when He led me to a small Bible the Gideon's left here. I opened it up to Psalms 138, 144–150 (amazingly enough!). If you read those chapters, there are many mentions of bad weather, rain, many waters, etc. God is sooooo very good. I WILL PRAISE THE LORD FOR HE IS GOOD!

After all of us had full stomachs and knew we were all okay, I gave Steve the keys to the little Chevy Malibu that was parked here since Friday. That was the only vehicle between our two families that survived Harvey! No AC, no CD player, only about eight inches off of the ground, but it was drivable, and they had to get out of Kingwood to a safe place. Our Christian Motorcycle Association (CMA) chapter in Porter, Texas, was all keeping tabs on us, and many invited us all to their homes, though for most we had no way of getting there, what with all the flooding and road closures everywhere you looked.

The president and vice president, a married couple, Bill and Melinda, had a home in Porter not too far from the hospital, and all the roads leading to their place were still open at this point. They invited us to come and stay with them, so that is where Steve went. They were going to stay the night and leave as soon as it was light to head to San Antonio where we had close family friends and who were completely out of any danger.

When they left, I went back to work, giving treatments to some of the remaining twenty-six patients that we did that day. I worked overnight that night without any breaks. We were getting patients from many hospitals that were flooding or just plain overloaded, so we were extremely busy. I did work that evening with a very discouraged patient. She was not cooperative, not happy, not allowing anyone to cheer her up, or be nice to us to say the least. She was the reason God had me there that day. That patient was just so ugh! That's the best way I can describe her. Ugh! I tried all my usual tricks—and after ten years of doing dialysis, I had quite a few—yet nothing worked. She was one tough patient!

Then I heard this very still small voice. What? Well, crazier things have happened! So I asked her, "Wanna play a game of Uno?"

She looked at me like I had lost my mind! She said yes just to get me to go away, she told me later. She thought she was calling my bluff. Hahaha! To quote Elmer Fudd and Bugs Bunny from Looney Toons, "She don't know me vewy well, do she?" I pulled out the game of Uno that I keep with me for just such occasions. We played a few games, which were her very first ever, and she won every single time. It was pathetic. She kicked my butt in every single one of those games! Playing those games broke down the massive walls she had built up in her life and around her heart.

God can do all things, and there is nothing impossible with Him! He used a simple children's game of Uno to blow those walls up to smithereens! I was able to minister to her and led her in the prayer of salvation. We talked for ages, and I called her the Lord's battle-ax and showed her in His Word, Jeremiah 51:20, that that was a good thing!

From that point on, that's what I called her! It was awesome what God did in her life in just those few hours of dialysis! *Wow!* I don't know if I've mentioned this, but I pray with every single one of my patients; and sometimes, if there's anyone (or many) in the room, I pray with them too before I leave that patient. When I prayed with her that evening, God gave me a special word of encouragement for her. It was so powerful!

At 9:09 a.m., I posted on Facebook,

> Day 6. Steve, Daniel, and Hannah are en route to San Antonio, tho instead of the usual three hr trip, it's going to be closer to 6–7. Tons of road closures and water over roads my little car won't make it thru. I finished my last pt this morning at 0030, got to bed at 0130, up and at it this morning at 0520. No power yet so CPAP isn't working so not getting much sleep. They said at my sleep study that for every hour I "sleep"(lay down with eyes closed feeling like I'm asleep) I am only getting about nine min of actual sleep… pretty tired. I can only imagine how loud my snoring is… poor people in the community room! Lol! Going to start making a list of the stuff lost for insurance claim, tho won't know exactly everything till we can get to our apt.
>
> It's funny how seeing something here at the hospital plops a visual of something "else" lost at home into my head. I don't think I have pix of everything insurance has covered, so I'll have to get a few hours and go thru my facebook stuff for pix of all I can find.
>
> All is well, God is good and still on the throne! Now we are also starting to brace for the second wave of Harvey's shenanigans. Pray for strength, real rest and continued Divine Appointments. Love you guys!

As soon as it was light Wednesday morning, Steve and the kids set off for what normally only takes about three hours to travel, which became an eight-hour trip. Almost every other road they took ended up blocked off or washed out, so they had to turn around and try the next road, and the next road, and so on. If they had string following them from where they started to where they finally arrived, it would've looked like a huge spider web.

While they were travelling, I was able to get a few hours of a sleep break, then back to work until about 11:30 Wednesday night, helping do treatments for the twenty-two patients that needed dialysis.

One of my dearest friends that God blessed us with Araceli contacted me that evening to see if I was going to have a day off since it had already been almost a full week. I told her I was going to be off on Thursday but had no vehicle to go anywhere, so I was planning to stay in and read or whatever. She decided that I had been there too long as it was, so she was going to pick me up and take me to help another woman at our church who'd been extremely affected by Harvey with seven feet of water in her home. I informed her that I was willing, but had nothing appropriate to wear as we had lost all but the few sets of scrubs, my sundress, and a pair of Shape-Up tennis shoes that I had with me. She said that those would be fine as we were going to help clean, and the guys would do any heavy stuff. She also said she'd take me to our church, which had donations from people from all over the area and around the country to help those of us Harvey survivors.

I got to my cot about 11:45 p.m. and was so excited to finally be allowed to be outside and actually away from the hospital that I was just about to tears. It's amazing how something so small and insignificant as *being* outside or feeling the sun or rain or breeze on your face can change your entire outlook on a day!

However, when we get so focused on those possibilities and not staying focused on the author and finisher of our faith, we take a huge risk of despair should anything happen to dash those "best laid plans of mice and men!" Yes, you guessed it. She was unable to get to the hospital. Every single possible route to Kingwood from anywhere was closed off. Kingwood was an island, and no one could come in or go out without a boat. God bless her loving heart! She tried and tried for over two hours to reach me but to no avail! I was off limits! She called me sobbing, telling me all the ways she had tried and almost got arrested trying to get to me so I could have a day away.

As I told her not to worry about it and that I was okay and I had things I can do to just hang out and relax here at the hospital, tears were pouring down my cheeks. Another day with no escape from Harvey, depression, sickness, loss, devastation, and not to mention the same clothes! Then Steve called, and the cell phone service was so choppy, it disconnected us! Salt in my wound! I fought despair for over an hour.

While the dialysis team was taking care of the twenty-two patients that Thursday, I moped around the community room, then to the chapel, and finally went to an area that had a bench outside with nice trees, plants, etc. to enjoy some peace and quiet and the *outside world*. I barely made it outside before my dam broke. I ran to the bench and sobbed and sobbed! My heart was so distraught, and I had no idea where so many tears had come from! God had done so many wonderful things and miracles during my time in this disaster, and *now* I was "losing it?" Wow!

The enemy of our souls knows us well, and he knows where and when and how to attack us to where it is most effective! All I can say is, "God, forgive me for my time of selfishness and the pity party I participated in." And then, sitting on that bench, I prayed. I asked God to show me that my staying again for another full day truly was His plan for me and to give me His strength to do it.

God is so good and He loves us so very much! When our hearts break, so does His; when we sob, He catches every single tear! Nothing we do is in vain if we do our best and do it for Him and to further His eternal kingdom! He sent a single hummingbird with such beautiful coloring to flit around me and the many plants and flowers in bloom around me. It went from flower to flower, then, to my amazement, he stayed not two feet from my face, looking at me with its little head tilted as if asking me, "Why are you crying, and why are you in such despair? Don't you know that God loves you? Why do you doubt? God knows everything you have need of and everything others need. Trust Him!"

Then it flitted to plants and flowers farther and farther away until he flew away. Amazing! I was able to get a few pictures, but as it was a hummingbird, it is a blur in most of them. As I'm writing this, I am once again overcome with His presence and remember clearly how He spoke to me that day.

That day, I had a few nurses hunt me down and thank me or working my magic on that extremely difficult patient. They said that they couldn't believe the drastic change on this patient; and when she noticed their timidity near her when they first went into her room, she told them, "God came in last night with Melody, the dialysis nurse, and totally changed my life!" To God be the glory, and I told them so. They were amazed! God's and "my" battle-ax ministered loudly to every single person that entered her room for the rest of the time she was in there. It was so awesome!

The post to Facebook at 8:46 a.m. was as follows:

> Day 7. I'm OFF today! Thank you Jesus! I'm getting picked up by a friend, Ara, and we'll be going to one of our church families home that flooded to help them start the clean up process. So many have lost everything. Ara is taking me to our awesome church sometime today to get some clothes and shoes and then I'll be back at the hospital tonight to be here working tomorrow.
>
> It is so amazing to see the work of the Spirit and be a part of touching so many. I was so bless last night when I went to check on a pt who had been so depressed and withdrawn the day before (I had told her that I would visit her the next day), so on my way to my cot at 10:30 ish, I went to her room. She was barely recognizable! The transformation of His touch was so awesome I just started crying. She saw me and started praising God and saying that God sent me to her. She had such joy and peace on her whole being, it was breathtaking! God is good! Another life won for His Kingdom! Hallelujah!"
>
> Another post at 1645: "Doing fine I heard Steve's voice this morning. MELTDOWN. Better now I have ANY down time to think about anything, then mini MELTDOWN. Missed lunch and, yup, MELTDOWN. BUT, during this meltdown I had gone outside quick to let it out and cried out to God as I flopped down onto a bench when this little hummingbird flitted by and hit every flower and bud all around me then sat himself on a branch to watch me for a bit. Such a beautiful little thing in life at just the right

time! Truly, "on the wings of a dove (or hummingbird) He sends down His love!!
Pray for His supernatural rest and strength."

Being there for seven solid days, I will tell you that the days start melding into each other. It starts to become a blur of activity, and patient care becomes endless. There was one night at the beginning of the week, either Monday, Tuesday, or Wednesday, that the administration was having an ice cream social for all the staff—every single one of us. Whether we were from housekeeping, maintenance, nursing, technicians, kitchen, security, or reception, all were invited to come and enjoy an ice-cream-type treat in the cafeteria after dinner was over at about 8:00 p.m.

I had a very full day and was late getting the machines out of a patient's room due to the dialysis technicians being busy elsewhere or gone, so I ended up missing dinner after having already missed lunch. I was very tired, frustrated, and hungry. Everyone was talking about getting ice cream, and all I wanted was real food! I was getting grumpy and could feel it.

As I pulled and pushed my two machines down the various halls, since I had my last patient in either the catheterization laboratory area, the 5500s, or the rehabilitation area, which is the 6600s, I had to bring them to a quick stop as the CEO Melinda was heading toward the cafeteria to serve the employees their ice cream and almost got squashed. She looked at me with her big smile and said to come on over to the cafeteria for some ice cream; but when I replied that I'd rather have real food, she cocked her head to one side and asked if I had dinner, to which I replied that I hadn't as I was just finishing with a patient, and the cafeteria is now closed. She asked where I was going with those machines, and I told her as I started moving them again. She told me to stay at the OBS storage unit where we kept the machines and most everything else at the time until she came for me. I agreed and barely got everything of mine situated in the storage when she was there telling me to follow her. I followed her but had no idea what she was working on. She led me to the administration offices area and into the conference room where she told me, "Help yourself and please have seconds! When you're done, come to the cafeteria for some hard-earned ice cream!"

She left me in front of a Rudy's Bar-B-Q buffet! They had chicken, ribs, sausages, beans, their creamed corn, biscuits; I think they had like a potato or macaroni salad too. I was actually served by two of the administrator guys, and they sat in there and chatted with me while I ate. When I was almost done, they left me to go help Melinda serve others and wait for me to get my ice cream! We had a great time, and I was treated very well. They helped me out of a hole that my fatigue and flesh was digging. It was another of God's many times that He picked me up and held me in His arms during this devastating time for our community and the separation of Steve and I.

There were so many times that God showed up and showed out! Those times were not just for me but for others to see Him, His goodness, His provision, His compassion, His protection, His mercy, His faithfulness, and His great love for each of us! God is so good!

On Thursday, I worked until about 6:00 p.m., most of that time in the ICU. By this time, I was the only staff member that had been there since the lockdown placed by Dialyspa the previous Friday and the day before the lockdown placed by Kingwood Medical Center. All other staff had been able to go home two to three days before. When I was putting the supplies, medicines, etc. away at the end of all treatments ordered for that day, the charge nurse Gemma B., RN asked if I informed the office (Dialyspa headquarters) about my home and situation. I told her not yet, to which she exclaimed, "*What*? You need to do it now! They need to be aware of your situation!"

She watched me jot a quick text to my supervisor Yvonne H., the boss Ismael R., and I think I cc'd the CEO/Founder, Dr. Jeff K., my situation. *Wow!* My phone blew up in seconds. I didn't know what that phrase meant until that moment. It got texts almost non-stop for a while. They were shocked to say the least. It seemed that some of our staff in the company in general had been affected by the hurricane, and some of the Dialyspa clinics were damaged, but no one had lost everything. They couldn't believe it, and they were astounded that I hadn't said anything until then. They asked why I hadn't told them sooner, and I replied that I had been extremely busy, my family was safe, and I had a cot at the hospital. The cot was ending the next night, however, and I was stuck; I had nowhere to go. They said they would get back to me. Within minutes, I was told I was definitely off the next day, Friday, and that Yvonne would be there to pick me up. Of course, I didn't get the texts about her being there until the next day as the cell service was still wacky, so when she called the next day to remind me that she was coming to get me, I was at my apartment sorting through stuff.

After I sent my message, I said goodbye to the staff who were finishing up for the day and headed to ICU where I had told one of the nurses Jennifer C. that I'd meet her up there at the end of her shift, about 7:15 p.m. or so. She was going to take me to see if there was access to our area yet. When I got up there, she asked if I was finally going home, to which I told her no, I wasn't, as I had no home to go to.

She about flipped out! She asked what I meant; and when I told her, she couldn't believe it! She asked where I'd been going at night, and I told her the community room where my cot is. She was ada-mant. "You are *not* going to that cot tonight! You are coming home with me and sleeping in a real bed! Good grief! I am so sorry you have had to sleep on a cot for a few days." She thought I had been staying with friends. When she found out it had been since the pre-vious Friday morning that I had been there, she marched me to the community room, left me to pack my few things to take with me to her place, and then she went to get her car and bring it to the closest door to the community room. A male nurse from Georgia helped me load up and carry my stuff out to her car. What a gentleman!

When we got out to her car, she was in tears. She felt so horrible about my being stuck in the community room and on a cot while she and the other nurses/staff were going home every night to a comfy bed. Bless her heart! She's like a kid sister to me, and I love that girl to pieces! So she packed me in the car, and we headed out. We were able to get to the area and even to our townhome.

It was one of the eeriest nights I can remember. It was completely dark. All power was out in that area because of the amount of floodwaters everywhere. There were cars in shrubbery, trees in places they don't belong, garbage, stuff already being placed at the side of the road that had been flooded; there were tables, chairs, dishes, house stuff in yards, roads, bushes, trees, everywhere! It was also eerily silent! Not a bug chirped; not a bird, cat, dog; nothing—absolute quiet!

As we turned the corner within the complex, I saw both my white Ford Explorer and our son and daughter-in-law's Chevy Equinox abandoned and covered in this grayish gunk. Our Explorer was actually parked *perfectly* in a parking spot, and the Equinox was in the bushes. We made two more turns and neared our townhouse. I started tearing up at the devastation that I saw. Suddenly, I smiled. Someone had placed a steel cross directly in front of our doorway! She stopped, and we tried to open the door, but it was swollen and wouldn't open.

As we got back into her car to go to her place, the maintenance man Alex walked up and gave me a hug. He told me that the next morning, there were about two hundred workers coming in to gut out the apartments and townhomes. *What?* They can't take anything out of our homes as insurance companies want pictures, and there just may be stuff that wasn't touched (yes, that was high hoping) and things that we could salvage. They have to give us a chance to go through it ourselves first! I told him that, and he replied that if we don't want them in our apartment, then we need to be there before they get there, and they are planning on being there at 8:00 a.m. I told him I'd be there by 6:30 but had no way of getting into our townhome, and he said he would meet me there and get me in. So I immediately called Steve and Daniel and told them and asked if there was any way they could be at the apartments by 7:30. They would try their best, but with all the road closures and detours, they couldn't promise anything. I would need to do the best I can to keep the apartments people free.

We left at that point, and Jenny took me to a little Mexican food drive-through for an amazing burrito and off to her home. On the way, she asked what, if anything, I was hoping to have survived Harvey in our home. I thought about it and, though I felt it to be a selfish miracle, I told her that there was a ship I had been blessed with many, many years ago, a replica of the HMS *Victory*, which was made from the same Black Forest of Germany wood as the actual ship that was key to defeating Napoleon and the French and Spanish armies way back in September 1805 and completely destroying any dreams he had left of invading and conquering England. It still, to this day, serves as Her Majesty's flagship—still seaworthy! The replica was a gift to me from some very dear friends in Washington state. God had told them to gift it to me as we had been going through some major trials and tribulations, and they immediately packed it up and brought it over to me. It was one of the things most sentimental to me, I think.

That couch was *so* comfortable! I slept like a log and had power for my CPAP the whole entire night! I woke up a little more rested than I had been for almost a week. We got up early enough to get ready, leave, and have me at the complex in time for her to be at work on time. However, when we arrived and Alex didn't show up, she stayed with me until I hunted down where Alex was staying, and he followed me to what was left of our townhome. I felt so bad that she was late getting to work, but she completely refused to leave me alone as there was looting happening everywhere, and she didn't want me to get hurt. Bless her heart! She is a very sweet and precious friend/ kid sister!

As promised, he got me into that townhome. He went in through the patio doors and came out through the front door. What a mess! I quickly found a paper plate in the bushes and wrote a note on it then ran it over to Daniel and Hannah's apartment and taped it to their door that said that no one was allowed to enter until either Daniel or Hannah Hall were present. Once I was back at our place, I started checking every room to see what was soaked and what had been spared. At about 7:45, Steve, Daniel, and Hannah pulled up! Hallelujah!

Daniel and Hannah ran off to their apartment and were able to open the door merely by using her key and then pushed with all their might to force the door open. While they were dealing with their stuff and assessing the damage, which was even more extensive than ours, we began the arduous task of picking through the debris that used to be our beautiful home. There was still a lot of water standing in our home, and nothing was where we had left it. As I went in and passed the entryway, I unwittingly glanced over to where I remembered my ship *Victory* had been.

It was *untouched*! The cabinet it was on had been slammed against the kitchen island, and the force caused the ship to topple. The mast hit the wall behind it, and it stayed there, tipped over. It should have fallen over and then down into the waves. Granted, it would have "died at sea" like ships should do, but there it was, dry and beautiful and holding a crystal cross from its doom as well! I couldn't believe it! Of course, I burst into tears and shouts of joy! Steve was shocked as well. He had told me earlier in the week not to expect to see it in one piece and prepare to have to throw it away, but nope! Yet again, HMS *Victory* defeated the odds!

Throughout the morning and over the next few days, Sam the police officer would stop by and check on us and make sure we were okay. He was worried when I was alone for those brief times while Steve went somewhere or was doing something because of all the looters. His presence really made us feel safe and secure and also gave any looters that were paying attention something to think about before they messed with us! Bless his heart; he was a stable rock of safety during this whole thing. He even checked on me once or twice while I was in lockdown in the hospital.

There was very little that was untouched and two thirds of what we thought was salvageable wasn't. So much of our stuff literally washed away, and what didn't went swimming in a sea of filth and unmentionable stuff. So with that huge relief, we did our best to open doors, drawers, cabinets, closets, containers, you name it. Most things were able to be opened and emptied, but there were some that we couldn't. I was so engrossed (*gross* doesn't even come close, pun intended) with our search and rescue efforts that I totally forgot that we live in Texas, where there were things like snakes and other creepy poisonous creatures around, and that they too had been flooded, and they went swimming like we did and landed in places that weren't necessarily their homes.

I was using my phone to get pictures of everything (ended up with 209 pictures total); and while trying to get pictures in the kitchen, I was in a few inches of water, trying to balance on the refrigerator that was leaning on its side against the laundry room and getting a picture of a lone knife in my knife block and Norwex dusting mitt when, as the flash happened, *things moved*. *Oofdah* (that's Minnesotan for "*holy buckets*")! Things in the water scattered when they saw the light flash and headed under the fridge!

Remember, at this point, there still was no electricity, and everything was dark except what light came in through the doors and muddy windows and our flashlights. I immediately thought about the various poisonous possibilities. I also started thinking of the likelihood of survival if bitten by one of those various poisonous possibilities! I screamed—yes, I did. I screamed like a little girl, and Steve came running. With both our lights on the area, we realized just exactly what was hiding in the water in my kitchen. I had *fish* in my kitchen! We couldn't believe it. We both cracked up in laughter, and he started teasing me about my not being hungry since there was sushi around! I still laugh when I think about it. Wow, fish!

The apartment complex management had asked everyone who was entering their homes to take anything you didn't want, was destroyed, etc. and pile it in the driveway, so we were creating quite the pile. I think I cried enough tears throughout the day to add at least an inch of water in the place! So much was lost that can never ever be replaced: a necklace that our oldest child, Mary had given me, goopy with filthy slime; a picture that our middle child, Bethany had painted; our youngest child Daniel's collage pictures kind of melded together, completely unusable; my dad's ship picture that my family had for more than forty years; my mom's Dake Annoted Reference Bible; and so much more—gone!

We were hard at work for a while and decided to check on Daniel and Hannah. We walked over and helped them for a few minutes, made sure she was doing okay as she was pregnant, then headed back to try to finish at least one room before we all took a lunch break. As we walked back to our townhouse a different route, we found some of our stuff. There was one of our patio chairs somewhat under the front end of their neighbor's car, my handmade wooden plant stand in the bushes about the distance of a block from our place, and some other odds and ends. It was like following Hansel and Gretel.

We were only gone about fifteen to twenty minutes total, but when we returned, we noticed some of our stuff that we thought we could salvage (another pile) was missing. We started noticing a few trucks driving along, super slowly and realized that many of them were probably casing the area and "shopping" at will. From that time on, we decided to keep someone outside all the time.

I asked Steve to help me carry a heavy object out to the "throw" pile; and once he left the front area, we heard a motor come close and stop close by. He went running out to the drive, and lo and behold, it was our good friend Javier from our CMA chapter! He had gone through an entire tank and a half of gas and spent hours to come over to help us! He had tried with his four-wheeled vehicle, but due to road closures, he went back and got his motorcycle and forged through the muck and mire to live the CMA motto of "Here When You Need Us!" Bless his heart!

That young man was there all day long and was such a tremendous help! Steve and Daniel had to leave to try to find a storage unit place that had available units, and while they were gone, he had come in to carry a box filled with some of my china that survived (I only lost about five pieces) outside when we heard another vehicle, which sounded like a truck, stop outside our door. He went running outside, and sure enough, there was a group of young guys looting! They saw him come around the entryway, ran to their truck, jumped in, and took off squealing their tires. He did come "packing," and I'm not just talking about boxes, if you know what I mean!

One thing about Texans in particular, the majority of them have these wonderful pieces of paper that allow them to conceal and carry firearms on their person, and most of those people really know how to use them! After all, Texas has a motto that states, "Come and Take It!" for a reason.

He was awesome! He helped us load everything we could onto a trailer and truck that more of our CMA chapter members allowed us to borrow; and while Steve and Daniel took it, unloaded it, came back, and finished loading what was left, Javier helped me pack up, sort, and open things we couldn't open earlier. We used everything we could find to pack up stuff: towels that had been up on a top shelf, throw blankets, paper towels, nasty T-shirts that we were hoping we could salvage with washing with some strong soap, just to name a few. We wrapped my china and my collection of lighthouses (I didn't lose even one of those) and teapots (I didn't lose any of those either, though there are a few that I will never be able to make tea in again due to some cracks or tiny holes in the sealed surface). While he helped, some stuff got carried off by looters. All in all, very little of the salvageable stuff was stolen. God is good! He not only protected some of the stuff that meant a lot to me, but He kept us safe as we sorted, salvaged, bagged, wrapped, boxed, and investigated what we could.

The apartment complex came along throughout the day to inspect the damage and the families that were now displaced and were so caring! They made sure we all had a place to stay, if we weren't able to stay there in the second or third floor units, and made sure they got all our information for communication in the days ahead.

Right after they went on their way to the next apartment/town-home, a van pulled up with a bunch of people. They all got out and started delivering a pizza or two to each of the homes that had someone there working. They said they were from one of the local churches and wanted to be sure we had food. What a blessing that was! We were able to feed our friend and ourselves after working so hard!

After a few more hours, as it was becoming dusk, the complex informed everyone that they had employed a security company to come in and watch our stuff that has been sorted through thus far so we could leave for the night and not worry about the things we'd been doing and hoping to save. What a relief! That had been on the forefront of our minds all afternoon.

Cell service was finally starting to function a little more like normal, and I was getting texts like crazy. My supervisor Yvonne had come to take me to my home in the late morning, but found that I was already there. She also had a prepaid credit card from her, Ismael, and Jeff from Dialyspa. They wanted to be sure I had a way to eat and feed my family during this time of displacement. It was such an amazing blessing, let me tell you! Then Ismael called me to see where we were staying from that point. I told him that we were staying at the same friend's house that had housed Steve, Daniel, and Hannah on Tuesday night; but after that night, we had nowhere planned. He texted me later and had made reservations at the very last hotel/motel room in the entire area (the next closest room available was way over in The Woodlands). He himself paid for us to stay there a week. I couldn't believe it! Of course, I started crying. The flood of help and thoughtfulness from those at the main office of Dialyspa was humbling and amazing. I work for such a great, local, and caring company!

We all headed to Bill and Melinda's home to get cleaned up. We were a disaster! We were muddy with…let's just call it "stuff"… from the knees down and on our shirts from picking up and moving items. Our shoes were completely destroyed, but we were going to continue to use them through this time of endless muck and mire. After we all got cleaned up, we took them out to dinner as a thank you for putting us up both of the nights that they did. We went to eat at a Mexican food restaurant in Porter. Once we smelled the aroma of cooking food, our mouths started to water; we were famished!

The next day, we hit the nastiness again. After working for a few hours, we got word that U-Haul and Penske were offering deals for anyone that was displaced by Harvey but was on a first come, first served basis. They also refused any cardboard boxes. Everything had to be in rubber totes, and those were extremely hard to find. Most stores were completely out of them as well as bleach, mops, shovels, Lysol, Pine-Sol, rubber gloves, baby bottle brushes, and pipe cleaners—anything for cleaning!

Steve took off to get a unit with Daniel while Javier (bless his heart; he came back for another day) and I continued sorting and getting stuff out. The guys were able to find some totes, but we only had some cleaning supplies that were donated to us while my family were refugees in San Antonio. We were able to borrow Bill's trailer and truck so we could move all our and Daniel and Hannah's stuff to a storage unit. So the rest of the day, the guys were loading and unloading that trailer and truck. No lunch was brought in by others that day, so we had the guys pick us up some Whataburger on their way home from the first load at the storage unit. We finished that day. Steve was not a happy camper at some of the stuff I wanted to try to salvage, but when you lose everything, what few things have even a remote chance of being salvageable, you grab it!

When we got to the motel that late afternoon, we were beyond nasty again. I couldn't stand how gross I was, so I started the long procession of people wanting to take a shower. I got in that shower with its wonderful hot water and just let it run over my body. I had my eyes closed, just relaxing with the nice pressure hitting my back, helping the day's stress wash away.

I opened my eyes and thought I caught some movement to my left. I started pulling the curtain and *oh my goodness!* There was a humongous cockroach on the curtain! I yelped, and we kind of stared at each other for a second. Then he did the unthinkable; he moved toward me! I screamed bloody murder, jumped out of that shower backward, and ran through the door into the main part of the room where Steve, Daniel, and Hannah sat on their beds talking. My poor kids saw way more of me than they ever imagined or bargained for, let me tell you! I just stood there, screaming and pointing to the shower saying, "Kill it! Kill it!"

Daniel starts busting out laughing and then teasing me about it before going in and squashing the nasty thing. He brought it out to show me it was dead, to which I responded with more screaming. Yes, he was being ornery because he could.

I finally had grabbed a towel to somewhat cover myself; but I tell you, between getting assassins for cockroaches and modesty, assassins for those things will always win! It's about my survival! I even had Steve go in there and verify there were no other critters of any kind in that bathroom before I moved a muscle. They tease me about imitating Goldie Hawn in the movie *Bird on a Wire* when she was taking a shower and the same-sized cockroach was on the show-erhead and ended up in her hair. I honestly don't have any idea how she was able to do that scene! My situation was completely unexpected and definitely unwanted, yet hers was totally scripted!

I still get creeped out just remembering that shower! To this day, I always check the shower and curtain before I get in or even start the water. Poor Hannah and Daniel will never forget that weekend in the motel with us. Oh well, we all have our issues and breaking points. They know mine is cockroaches! I don't want to leave a bad impression of that motel with anyone, so I'm not mentioning the name of it, but let me just say that humans were not the only things that had their homes flooded. There were critters of all shapes and sizes that were seeking refuge and a place that was dry and safe from the flood waters. I think every dry place had critters of some kind in them.

For the rest of that week, we would get a couple of totes from the storage unit and start cleaning, scrubbing, and disinfecting each and every thing—one at a time—until our hands were raw. We had to get stuff from the unit, bring it to the motel, clean, dry, and rebox, then take it back and get the next few boxes. By the end of the week, the totes would stink so bad, we had to open them outside of the room and dump any water that was in them out before bringing the tote in to be cleaned. We had to scrub the totes too. A friend of mine at the hospital, another ICU RN named Cindy, knew I had lost all of my Young Living Essential Oils, and that I had to scrub all that stuff and how bad it stunk; she brought me a box of stuff to help. She is a Doterra distributor, and that sweet lady gave me a diffuser and some oils to help us not get sick from inhaling that nasty mold and filth from the floodwaters. What a special, wonderful blessing!

By the middle of that week, I had to return to work, and we continued living in a hotel/motel for the next six and a half weeks. We were in one hotel for three weeks, and I tried to have a game night to help kids in the hotel have a little fun since they were all cooped up in their hotel rooms and very rarely able to get outside and be kids. Just a couple of little ones showed up, so I provided snacks, and we played a couple of action games. The family that had kids show up were very appreciative, but since those two kids were the only ones that came; and as I was working full time again and still doing the cleaning stuff, that was the only time I did it.

We moved to a less expensive hotel at the end of that week, anyway, which is where we stayed until we were able to get into an apartment. Several people from our *amazing* church Crossroads Fellowship Kingwood would leave us home-cooked meals at the church; and when they did, they would text or call me and let me know so I would go after work or during the day and pick it up and take it home to our hotel. It helped so much and helped us feel the love so many had for us during this time! God bless every single one of them!

All the weight we had lost during the spring and summer swimming every day and working out at the fitness center at our townhome complex returned with friends by the end of our hotel/motel life. Steve would go to every apartment complex in the Kingwood area to see if they had any one-bedroom apartment coming available as soon as possible. Every complex was full and had a waiting list. It got so discouraging! Talk about cabin fever! We had it bad!

One day, when I came home from work, Steve said he had a surprise for me. Well, he changed it to a two-fold surprise. He had me close my eyes, and when he let me open them, I was looking at a Mr. Coffee espresso machine! Woo-hoo! I was ecstatic! I made some espresso right then and there—for the one and only time in the hotel,

I might add. I learned one thing that day: do *not* use powder-flavored creamer for a latte ever!

That said, however, it was the first homemade latte I'd had since a few days prior to Harvey. So for the rest of the time in the hotel, I had espresso, no lattes. He was so proud of himself for finding that machine for me. It was exactly like the first one he had ever bought me when we had lived in Yelm, Washington.

After I tried to enjoy my hotel-made latte, I remembered he had said he had a two-fold surprise. I asked him what the second one was, to which he replied, "I found us an apartment that we can move into on October 14!" That was the best news I had heard in a while! He had them show him pictures as no apartment was available for viewing; every apartment in Kingwood was full for that matter, and he signed for it right then and there, sight unseen for the most part. It was a one bedroom/one bathroom and included a washer and dryer. Then he let the other shoe fall, so to speak. It was on the second floor. Ugh! Stairs! I hate stairs! He hates stairs! We really, really hate stairs!

The disappointment lasted only about ten seconds as, bottom line, we had a real home soon! No more hotel/motel living! We can cook, do dishes, and have a separate room for sleeping, entertaining, eating, etc.! We were almost home! It was the end of September, so only about three weeks to go. Hallelujah!

On September 22, 2017, at 10:00 p.m., I posted on Facebook,

> It's beginning to feel a little more like home…
> Steve found an espresso machine just like the 1st
> one he ever bought me today at a thrift store and
> bought it. I tried it out and everything works and
> it tastes great! I love my Honey! Hotel or not, the
> coffee is great now!!

On September 22, 2017, at 11:46 p.m., I posted,

> If you have a man in your life who helps bring
> balance to your world, who isn't perfect but he's
> perfect for you, who works hard and would do

anything for you, who makes you laugh until you cry, but drives you crazy, who is your best friend and sometimes your only friend, who you want to grow old with who you are thankful for and truly adore, let him have a moment and put this as your status.

(Copy paste and add a picture)

Unfortunately, I have no pictures of us anymore. They were all destroyed by Hurricane Harvey. BUT, we know what we look like and so do ya'll!! It's all good!! We'll get some more photo opps! :0}

When October 14 came, we moved in, and it only took about two hours to get everything brought in and placed where it was supposed to be. We had a new bed from Skero's Furniture and headboard and frame that we got a really great deal on. Skero's was discounting their furniture for anyone who had been displaced by Hurricane Harvey. The bed was exactly like the nice one we lost in Harvey with massage and head/feet elevating abilities. When we tested it out at the store, we almost fell asleep right then. That first night in our apartment, let me tell you, we both slept like babies! That was a wonderful night. Now we can start getting back to a normal life, like the one we had before Hurricane Harvey came in to disrupt things— well, as normal a life as our lives can be!

God knows the desires of our hearts, and He cares about even what we would consider the little things, things like a little ten-dollar espresso maker, or a bed of our own! He didn't have to bless us with those things, but He did because He loves us! He wants us to know and feel that love, and He wants others to see it and hear about His love from those who have it. We talk to people every day, everywhere we go; and when good or bad things happen to us, we tell others about it. How awesome it is to be able to tell others what a wonderful, caring God we serve! He promises that He will take everything that happens to us—all our trials, our experiences, our situations—and work them together for our good and for His glory (Romans 8:28)!

He also says in His Word that when we serve and follow Him, He will preserve and bless us for our good always (Deuteronomy 6:24).

As much destruction and disruption Hurricane Harvey caused, the devil didn't win anything in it. God brought so much of His glory and might; it was awesome! He broke down walls and shattered chains of color, race, political views, and generational prejudices. He brought so many people together that had been at odds with each other and people that had hurts and distrust of others that it was glorious! God is good all the time! All the time, God is good!

CHAPTER 15

Home on a Dead Battery!

So today, Tuesday, July 24, 2018, I was coming home from being at the Bridge Crest Nursing Home church service our church holds there. Steve and I go there and sing and fellowship with those wonderful people that are unable to get out and attend any church on Sunday. I had to take the West Lake Houston route home because I had to stop by the Kingwood post office to put a hold on our mail for the time I would be up in Minnesota getting Steve, finishing getting our house ready for sale, then driving a moving truck back down here to Texas.

Anyway, after I left the post office, I heard a different sound in my car; and suddenly, my AC was out, but the fan was still blowing. As I began to pull over to turn off the engine to see if it will fix when I restarted it, I heard a voice tell me to not stop or turn off the engine but to go straight home. Of course, I kept heading toward home.

The closer I got to home, the more lights were coming on in my dashboard and less and less things were working! I noticed my blinkers weren't working, and I started to wonder if any of my lights were working, though I highly doubted it! As I turned onto the I-59S feeder road from Northpark Drive, the white truck next to me on the left almost hit me coming into my far right lane. My horn didn't work, and I had no to place to go! Thank God the driver realized I was there and straightened up his truck! Whew! Barely missed me!

It was then that I realized that my power steering wasn't working now either. When I tried to turn onto Kellington Drive by my apartment complex from the feeder road, I had to really pull that steering wheel to get the car to turn, and it felt like everything died once I passed the turn, so I hit the gas; and by some miracle, it kept going. One more right turn into my complex and then another right turn into the gate to find a parking spot and I'd be done.

Well, I got into the gate, and as I was turning left into the first available parking spot on the left, it gave up the ghost! Now, not only was I blocking two vehicles in the parking spots but was sticking in the driveway. There was nothing to do but push it into the spot because all of my attempts to restart it were fruitless. I pulled hard on the gear handle, and it wouldn't let me get it into neutral for several attempts. I finally got it to go into neutral and had that steering wheel yanked as far over as possible but had to push the car alone.

I got it backed up at the correct angle and was getting into the spot when I hit an issue. The last half of the spot was at an incline! *Ugh!* As hard as my legs were moving, my car wasn't! I was giving it my all to no avail when a black man pulled his car into park when he pulled into the gate and saw me. Next thing I know, my car goes zooming into place, and I almost fell on my face! I hollered, "Thank you very much!" to that gentleman.

And he said, "No problem! Glad I could help."

I jumped in to hit the brake as it was starting to roll backward after getting to the end of the spot, and when I got out to properly thank him, he was gone! No car or man anywhere to be seen. Praise God! I laughed out loud at the devil and said, "See, devil? This attack on my car did nothing but give God another opportunity to be glorified and another person to be blessed! Hahaha, devil! You can't have my joy! God is still on my side, and *nothing* you do can prosper against me!" That's God's word in Isaiah 54:17.

That night, he tried again by our garbage disposal's not working while I was about ready to go to bed, so I had to stay up to ensure it didn't overflow as I was doing a load in the dishwasher, which drains into that sink. Even then, it just gave me more time to glorify and worship God! I was able to crank up the praise and worship and write this out so as not to ever forget God's faithfulness and how He raises up a standard against the enemy when he comes at us like a flood (Isaiah 59:19)! Hahaha! To God be the glory!

The brother of Jesus, James, tells us in his New Testament book to count it all joy when we end up in various trials (James 1:2–4). This day had more than its fair share of those, let me tell you! You know what, though? As I hit each one of those trials head-on and with joy, I felt His strength and peace flood over me like never before. It was kind of like how I imagine it felt for Aaron when Moses poured the anointing oil over his head, and it dripped down everything all the way to the ground: warm, gentle, soothing, good-smelling oil just oozing over you. He is so good, and His faithfulness never ever fails!

CHAPTER 16

Biker Initiation

Steve and I wanted to ride on this gorgeous Friday, October 5, 2018, as I was off. Steve had a job interview with Aldi's Grocery Store on Kingwood; and when he got back, I woke up. It was about 8:40 a.m., so I showered, got dressed, and had some of my cooked mixed grains with milk and sugar for a hearty breakfast. We got out and hit the road at 10:00 a.m.

As we were filling up the gas can, we were notified that a member of our CMA chapter was in need of some help, so we went and helped Tom load his *big* Harley Davidson motorcycle onto his rented trailer, then headed out on a very long ride on our bikes. I rode the 2013 Honda Shadow, and Steve rode the 2010 Can-Am. The reason for the ride was fourfold:

1. We needed to find out exactly how many miles the Shadow got per tank of gas.
2. I needed to practice riding in lineup on the Shadow.
3. I needed practice riding the Shadow.
4. We needed to rid ourselves of some stress that was building all week.

We ended up at Vernon's BBQ on the 105 in Conroe, Texas, for lunch. That was wonderful! They had a great variety of foods on the menu, including fantastic burgers (Steve had the bacon cheeseburger), fajita tacos (I had the chicken fajitas special with tamale and beans), and barbecue stuff. They even had smoked turkey! I had to try their home-dipped onion rings with zesty sauce—*divine!* We enjoyed the environment and friendly service as well as huge variety of customers.

From there, we headed north on 105 until we got to Montgomery, Texas, and took a right on the 1097 to the 1725, then on the 1484. Just as we were about to turn left on the 105 to head toward Cleveland, we were at the stoplight by the very *little* town called Cut and Shoot, Texas, with at least one car in front, then a semitruck loaded with pipes, then me on the Shadow, Steve on the Can-Am, and a Toyota Prius hybrid. The light turned green, the semi started to move, so I let off the brake, and then I heard a crunch and Steve holler. Next thing I know, I get shoved forward and lurched to the right. The handlebar shoved into my chest, and I braced my fall with my right hand/arm twisting to keep from being shoved into the metal of my bike. My left knee twisted around, but I was okay.

Steve was up running to me and checking me out and said he was okay. After he helped me up, I double-checked joints and body parts on both of us then headed to the car to check them out. The woman was already out of the car to check on us but was shaking like a leaf. She had two kids in the car with her. They all seemed to be okay. No one had hit their head, was bleeding, or broke any bones apparently. Come to find out, she didn't have any insurance and stated that she was homeless but was actually en route to put a deposit down on an apartment. She stated she worked at the Conroe ISD as a custodian.

I was able to pray with her while the three different police officers were putting their notes together. She told the police that she had her foot on the brakes and was stopped until suddenly, she wasn't. She hit Steve at about twenty-five to thirty miles per hour, which shoved him almost two car lengths into me. If the light hadn't turned green and the semi wouldn't have started moving, I would've been shoved into the pipes and probably been skewered in the head. If the Can-Am didn't have the trailer hitch, Steve wouldn't be here today. The constable kept looking at the hitch and then to her front end and told Steve that the hitch had saved his life.

All of us kept searching for the back panel of the Can-Am that had the license plate on it but to no avail. It was gone! So after the highway patrol officer gave us all the paperwork we were supposed to get, he said we were free to go. I hopped on the Can-Am and headed to the nearest restroom. As I rode, however, I noticed there was a weird rubbing sound on the back tire. I prayed all the way there for God to not let the Can-Am be too damaged to drive. When I got back on the bike to go back to Steve, I had it in reverse and noticed that noise even worse, and then I heard a *thud*, like something falling onto the ground, and then a *crunch* when I ran over it. Uh oh! I killed the engine and jumped off and ran to the back. Well, I found the panel with license plate on it! It had been shoved up above the tire in the wheel well. I picked up all the pieces and set them in the "frunk," which is the trunk in the front of the Can-Am, like the old Volkswagen Beetle cars.

So she ended up getting two tickets. And after our friend Dan and Steve loaded our Shadow onto his trailer while I was directing traffic, we left, and she was still trying to find a person to tow her car and give her a ride. I pray she comes to truly know Him and His love and grace.

When we got home, Steve looked at me and said, "Well, honey, you are a true 'biker chick' now. You've had your first accident! You've been initiated!" Thank God we are okay! Had she hit Steve just ten seconds earlier, I would've been skewered. Those oil drilling pipes would've been through my face and out the back of my head. We only ended up with bruises, bumps, and being sore; but we are good, and God is amazing! Thank You, Jesus, for Your protection over us!

CHAPTER 17

Miscellaneous Acts of God

One day, while in high school, I wasn't feeling very well and had to walk the mile and a half home from school. It was in the spring, and we had been having a lot of thunderstorms, and it was looking more and more ominous with every step I took. I looked up at the clouds and prayed simply, "God, I don't want to get wet! Please don't let it rain on me or my stuff! Thank You!" It rained all the way home, but about two to three feet behind me! When I had to stop at a red light, the rain stayed in its place behind me! The second I got under the shelter of the carport at home, it deluged! Thank You, Jesus! His Word promises that if we ask anything in His name in faith, we will have what we ask (Matthew 21:22, Mark 11:24).

One night, Daniel was having a very hard time sleeping. He had nightmare after nightmare all night long. Sometime in the wee hours of the morning, he came to our room and to my side of the bed. He woke me up and asked to sleep with us and told me why. As I roused more, I felt this horrible, oppressive cold invade my room. I turned over and saw this demon coming into our room. I sat straight up and commanded him, "Leave right now in the name of Jesus! You have no authority or place here. We are children of the King of kings and the Prince of Peace, and you can't cross that blood-washed line! Now leave! Go back to the pit where you came from!" Once I started to pray, that thing froze and glared at me. You could've felt the hate and cut it with a knife; it was so thick. When I took authority over it, he couldn't leave fast enough! Daniel saw the whole thing too. He said that was the thing he kept dreaming of in his nightmares. He slept with us the rest of the night. The next time he had a nightmare and since, he prayed and took authority over whatever it was in the dream, and the dream changed to a good regular dream. Jesus has given us His authority and invites us to utilize it and walk in victory!

Another time, Mary was about fourteen or fifteen years old and wasn't feeling well. We all went somewhere and left her home alone. While we were gone, she was sleeping on the couch, and someone tried to open the front door. She woke up, and they did it again. It scared her really bad, so she started to pray for God to protect her and get whoever it is gone. Suddenly, two huge angels walked in the house and stood by the door! They were so bright, she had to shield her eyes. They were both wearing robes of white with gold sashes and holding massive flaming swords. They had long wavy hair and rippling muscles like she'd never seen before. What happened to the jokers on the other side of the door? She heard them running away, vehicle doors slamming, an engine rev, and the vehicle speed off into the night. We never had another problem with possible break-ins. Go figure!

$\mathcal{M}$elody Hall has been married to the love of her life, Steve, for over thirty-two years. She is the mother of three wonderful grown children with five wonderful grandchildren, who are spread out in two states Minnesota and Texas.

She is a dialysis registered nurse working for two different dialysis companies, a second generation ordained minister, and is very active in the Christian Motorcyclists Association and her local church Crossroads Fellowship in Kingwood, Texas. She is part of the altar/ prayer team.

She loves to spend time playing games of all kinds with family and friends; loves riding on her own motorcycle with her husband and friends; loves to be in nature, especially at the ocean or in the woods; read and write, sing for patients and ministry events. She is an inspirational speaker and exceptional friend, and she shows love to everyone she meets. She is involved in ministry at a local nursing home as often as her schedule allows.

She is originally from Southern California and has lived in seven states, four of which at least twice, and has moved a total of over thirty times. She collects lighthouses, teapots with character, and crosses. She loves making lattes and other coffee and tea drinks for herself and her friends. She is an avid "oiler," using essential oils for over seven years. She is a cancer survivor of two and a half years.

Her first publication was a children's story in Tucson, Arizona, when she was nine. This is her first published book.

Printed in the USA
CPSIA information can be obtained
at www.ICGtesting.com
LVHW050340050924
789975LV00019B/516

9 781098 025137